The Deadly Dog Training Myth

Cover & Book Design by Rachael Letendre

Eric R. Letendre
Visit my website at EricLetendre.com

The Deadly Dog Training Myth

Why the "experts" make it *impossible* to train your dog... and what you can do about it.

Eric R. Letendre

TABLE OF CONTENTS

INTRODUCTION

WARNING: This book will be shunned, vilified, and given bad reviews on Amazon. It will take courage for some of you to read it, so before you continue, let me ask a few questions:

1. Does your dog drag you down your street?
2. Does your dog tackle you and your guests?
3. Does your dog blow a gasket when another dog approaches on leash?
4. Does your dog steal food off your counters and tables?
5. Does your dog steal socks, underwear and anything else he can fit his jaws around?
6. Does your dog bolt out your door the second it opens?
7. Does your dog chew your furniture and anything else he can get his jaws on?
8. Does your dog dig holes big enough to break and ankle?
9. Does your dog run in the other direction when you say "come?"
10. Does your dog bark and won't stop when you say quiet?

And the even more important follow up questions:

- Have been told you can ONLY use positive reinforcement to solve behavior problems?
- Have you been told you must redirect, manage, ignore, and give your dog treats for any problem?
- Have you been made to feel guilty your dog is out of control?
- Have you spent weeks and weeks, maybe months; maybe even YEARS trying to fix your dog's obnoxious behavior?
- Have you worked with one, two, or maybe even more highly recommended "professional" dog trainers with little to no improvement?

If you have, then you are a VICTIM!

You are a victim of… **THE DEADLY DOG TRAINING MYTH**, which was created and is perpetuated by what I like to call, the *Church of Positive Only Training* (or the PO'd Church for short).

Let me warn you in advance, this is a powerful church with forceful and vengeful high priests and priestesses who do not take kindly to anyone who speaks out against their dogma. In a nutshell, they preach you are never allowed to use, or even think of using, any type of negative consequence, even the word NO, to bring your dog's behavior under control. Anyone using or suggesting negative consequences is labeled as abusive, mean, outdated, unscientific, and uneducated.

Legions of dog trainers who worship at the altar of the Church of Positive Only Training will come out hard against this book and try to convince you what I am going to share is false, wrong, dangerous, unscientific, cruel, abusive, and even inhumane.

The good news is I am not writing this book for them. As Mr. Wonderful on Shark Tank loves to say, "*They are dead to me.*" BUT NOT YOU! You and your dog are NOT dead to me. I want to help you. I want you to know there is hope and you CAN put an end to your dog's annoying and even dangerous behaviors. You've made a wise decision to read this book because in it, I will lay out another approach that provides you with a safe, peaceful, and humane way to communicate with your dog.

The reason you answered yes to any (or all) of those questions I just asked is probably because you've gotten poor results from "All Positive" training methods. This is NOT YOUR FAULT. It's simply because you CANNOT stop, reduce, or eliminate a behavior with rewards and reinforcement.

"All Positive" sounds nice, but it doesn't work to stop unwanted behavior, and it is very dangerous for your dog, which I'll prove in this book.

This may sound unimaginable, but if your dog is exhibiting behaviors you would like extinguished, please have a little faith and hang in there with me because in the following pages, I am going to show you once and for all how to finally STOP the annoying behaviors you've been living with.

Every week I work with thirty to thirty-five private dog training clients who are typical dog owners, just like you. These are real families with real dog problems. At least twice a week, I get calls from owners on the verge of giving up. They are going to either bring their dogs to the shelter or put their dogs to sleep. Often, when I meet with these people, they are in tears telling me how much they love their dogs but feel they must find them new homes because of bad behavior. Many have already worked with a trainer (or two) but are still having problems. They are not bad dog owners; they are victims of the Church of Positive Only Training's **DEADLY DOG TRAINING MYTH**.

This church has put your dog into a dangerous position. Dogs are in danger because when a dog's behavior is NOT brought under control, when a dog is aggressive, jumping, stealing, digging, biting, barking non-stop, pulling on leash, or doing any dozens of other undesirable behaviors, there's a good chance that dog will end up at the local (overcrowded) shelter and probably not make it out. According to the ASPCA, approximately 1.2 million shelter dogs are euthanized each year.

I work hard, each and every week, to decrease that number, one dog at a time, and I wrote this book for you, the average dog owner who's having some trouble ending unwanted behaviors, so you can also avoid the **DEADLY DOG TRAINING MYTH**.

I will show you how behavior works, how to TEACH your dog to perform desirable behaviors, and most importantly, how to STOP your dog from doing undesirable behaviors. My techniques may be controversial, but they are rooted in the principles of behavior, and are safe and effective. The choice to follow them is always one hundred percent yours.

THIS BOOK COMES WITH THREE REQUIREMENTS

1. You must have a sense of humor. Everyone seems to be so easily offended these days. I'll tell you upfront, I am not a PC kind of guy so if you don't have a sense of humor, you might not want to continue reading.

2. You have to live with a firm sense of reality. Dogs are wonderful animals that enrich millions of lives around the world; however, they are also predatory, capable of killing and seriously injuring people. If you can only think of dogs as furbabies running through fields of daisies and sunflowers, and if you think dog training is all sunshine and rainbows, you may need to put this book down. I take my job as a dog trainer seriously and look at dogs for what they are. Dog training has to be approached with a firm sense of reality.

3. You must keep an open mind. I've read, *"How to Win Friends and Influence People,"* many times, but I don't think that book will help garner me any friends in the dog training world. To quote the great Dale Carnegie, *"When dealing with people, let us remember that we*

> *are <u>not</u> dealing with creatures of logic. We are dealing with creatures of emotion, creatures bristling with prejudices and motivated with pride and vanity."*

I know dogs are a highly emotional topic. This is why a large group of dog trainers (The Church of Positive Only Training) has developed an ideology which sounds wonderful but in reality is dangerous to dogs. They are impossible to reason with and will attack me and this book. So, my advice is to keep an open mind and think about what I have to say. Watch the videos on the links I have provided as proof what I share works and will not turn your dog into a horned, snarling, out of control beast. Know I only have one goal:

To help you train your dog without harm, ideology, or opinion. I share only what works and the choice to follow my advice is always yours.

CHAPTER 1

"There are two ways to be fooled: One is to believe what isn't true. The other is to refuse to accept what is true."

Soren Kierkegaard

Would You Pay Someone $10,000 To Kill You?

Why ONLY Positive Reinforcement Is Dangerous

Three Spiritual Warriors died on October 8, 2009. Nearly sixty people had gathered together for a "Spiritual Warrior" retreat in Sedona, Arizona. Their $10,000 admission fee included head shaving, the "Samurai Game," which required them to play dead, and a thirty-six-hour desert meditation without food or water. The retreat ended with attendees entering a sweat lodge. As they entered, new age guru, James Arthur Ray, said, "*You are not going to die. You might think you are, but you are not going to die.*" As the tarp lowered, the ceremony began.

The heat inside the lodge escalated to two hundred degrees. People started to get sick. They began to vomit, hallucinate, and pass out. The guru told his attendees to disregard any physical problems they were experiencing. He told them to "stay positive" and to ignore signs of heat stroke. Positive thoughts would overcome any danger or discomfort.

Fifty-five people went into the sweat lodge that day. Fifty-two survived it. Three died from overheating and nineteen others were hospitalized after they collapsed or fell unconscious. James Arthur Ray was convicted of negligently causing the deaths of Kirby Brown, 38, of Westtown, New York, James Shore, 40, of Milwaukee, Wisconsin, and Lizbeth Neuman, 49, of Prior Lake, Minnesota.

The people who entered the sweat lodge were told to pay no attention to the negative consequences of the temperature inside. By ignoring and staying positive, three people paid with their lives. Nineteen others were hospitalized. Their guru was telling them to hang in there, but when something unpleasant happens, there's a good chance it is providing critical information to help you STAY SAFE!

USING ONLY POSITIVE REINFORCEMENT IS DANGEROUS FOR YOUR DOG

This story illustrates why ***ONLY*** positive reinforcement is dangerous. I didn't say positive reinforcement is dangerous. My point is ***ONLY*** positive reinforcement is dangerous. It's dangerous to any living thing on the planet. Both positive and negative consequences provide feedback. In some situations, this is information that can keep you alive.

So, why the huge push to use ***ONLY*** positive reinforcement in dog training? There is a mass movement, started in the 1990's, which seems to gain momentum daily, and with the advancement of the internet and social media, it does everything it can to make sure you train according to its dogma. It is the Church of Positive Only Training. Many of its true believers live in a dream world where their ideology is more important than results, even more important than your dog's life. More and more dog trainers have started pushing an all positive, force-free agenda, which is dangerous for your dog and this book will prove it.

Some people will attack me for what I share in these pages, so let me make it as clear as I can. I am NOT saying positive reinforcement is dangerous. I am saying ***ONLY*** positive reinforcement is dangerous, and your dog may pay the price if you try to train with ***ONLY*** positive methods.

NEGATIVE CONSEQUENCES KEEP YOUR DOG SAFE

At some point in your dog's life you must introduce a negative consequence; otherwise your dog could get lost, injured, or killed. There are two types of behavior which can end your dog's life and they both occur naturally.

First, dogs can unknowingly do things that are just plain dangerous. In fact, puppies remind me a lot of my young son. He seems to be on a constant suicide mission. Every time I turn around, he is on top of a table, climbing a staircase, or sticking something disgusting in his mouth. It's the same with puppies. They will chew electrical cords, eat anything, and will run out the door into traffic.

The second type is what you would consider "bad" behavior. Dogs will jump, steal food off your counter, poop on your rug, and eat trash. More often than not, this will put them in hot water with their human families. If it happens too frequently and if the human family can't bring these behaviors under control, the dog could make a trip to the local, overcrowded shelter. Left there long enough and you know what happens next.

Or, your dog may spend years stressed out beyond belief. One client I worked with had a very reactive jack russell terrier and spent five years trying to fix this problem with a veterinary behaviorist. FIVE YEARS! Patience is important when you are training a dog but five years is a lot of patience. This dog owner was a saint. His dog would lose it every time another dog came within a couple hundred feet of him. The veterinary behaviorist spent five years unsuccessfully trying to use treats to bring his behavior under control around other dogs. Think of the stress this dog and owner went through for five years because an "expert" said no negative consequences were allowed.

By the time I was hired to help, the dog was nine years old. In one session we taught him to calm and focus on his owner in the presence of other dogs. He's now taking daily walks at the park and has successfully completed a group training class. I know it may seem like I am bragging, but please watch the videos on my website, DeadlyDogTrainingMyth.com.

So, at some point in your dog's life, you must introduce and use some type of aversive if you really want your dog to be safe because positive reinforcement has its limitations. Positive reinforcement will NOT stop a dog from bolting out the door to chase a squirrel. If just a treat worked to get your dog back, you wouldn't need this book. But here's the reality. Running out your door and chasing squirrels is much more exciting and interesting than any treat you can offer. I don't care if you have steak, hot dogs, cheese, or freeze dried liver. So if that squirrel runs right in front of a car, all the positive reinforcement in the world isn't going to save your dog's life, but, a negative consequence could stop your dog from getting crushed. Personally, I would much rather apply an unpleasant consequence and stop the dangerous behavior than see a dog get injured or killed.

I know this is blasphemy. Positive reinforcement is pushed as the only method that can be used to train a dog, and in my world, anyone who steps up and does not promote the all positive agenda is painting a huge bullseye on his back. Everyone and their mother will take aim and knock down the person who would make such an outrageous statement. So let me make it crystal clear again. Positive reinforcement is awesome, great, and hands-down, the best way to TEACH behaviors. But, if you want to STOP a behavior, you must use some type of negative consequence.

When a dog trainer says he has to use a negative consequence to stop a behavior, the all positive, force-free crowd goes out of its mind, wrings its collective hands, and holds conferences and meetings of which the sole purpose is determining ways to stop mean abusive trainers who are out there harming dogs. And nothing could be further from the truth. I am making the case you should use both positive and negative consequences so your dog learns how to live with you and you with your dog.

There are millions of dogs safely contained in their yards with Invisible Fences (negative consequence), and no matter what your personal feelings might be, you have to agree they work. Gravity has taught me to be careful when I'm on a roof. Hot pans have taught me to protect myself when cooking. Most of these lessons were learned very quickly and have helped keep me safe. This is exactly what I want for your dog. I want your dog to be safe. If your dog has to be put in discomfort for a split second, I would much rather do that than sell you a bunch of pseudo-science based psychobabble about how you can only use positive reinforcement to train because both positive and negative consequences are needed to learn. You MUST develop a plan that incorporates both positive AND negative consequences.

COMMUNICATE WITH POSITIVE & NEGATIVE CONSEQUENCES

Dog training requires an understanding of behavior so you can effectively use both positive and negative consequences to communicate information to your dog. When you train a dog, a series of consequences are applied which can either increase or decrease the frequency of a behavior. Any trainer telling you to only use positive consequences is giving you an incomplete picture. So much BS is pushed on dog owners, it's crazy.

Dog training boils down to one word: COMMUNICATION. For years we have called it obedience training but it would be better if we started calling it communication training. The best way to communicate to your dog is through markers, which I will go into in more detail in Chapter 8. For now, a marker is simply a word paired with a consequence (positive or negative) that communicates to your dog what is expected of him. Training with markers helps pinpoint a behavior so your dog learns much faster. Once your dog understands a marker, you have effective communication. It may take a little while for your dog to initially learn markers, but once mastered, you'll be able to communicate to him for the rest of his life.

And if for some reason you think I am a guy who does not use positive training methods, let me make it very clear. I have been teaching dog owners the benefits of positive reinforcement for years and have seen first-hand how fast dogs can learn to perform behaviors if they are motivated. If you and I were to work together, we would spend ninety-five percent of our time using positive reinforcement to teach behaviors. Positive reinforcement is great for TEACHING behaviors. If you are teaching your dog to SIT, STAY, DOWN, COME, GIVE PAW, or perform tricks, positive reinforcement and treats are the way to go. Positive reinforcement will make behaviors much stronger. It is a great way for your dog to learn. It is a great way to teach. Your dog will be a happy student and will enjoy the process. But you must understand there is a BIG difference between teaching behaviors and STOPPING behaviors.

POSITIVE REINFORCEMENT CAN'T STOP A BEHAVIOR

A lot of dog trainers are guilty of wishful thinking. They wish dog training could be one way because they do not like the thought of having to use any type of negative consequence. I spend a great deal of time wrestling with well-meaning but misinformed "experts". In the past few months, I have been kicked out of two different shelters and called on the carpet by two different veterinarians.

The first shelter gave me the boot after helping a German shepherd puppy with serious food bowl aggression. If you approached his bowl, this six-month-old puppy would growl, and then attack. Within five minutes I was able to walk up, take his food bowl away from him, and then hand it back without problem. With some follow through, I know this puppy could have accepted people around his bowl. Unfortunately, the shelter personnel did

NOT like my technique to STOP food bowl aggression because it provided a negative consequence. This puppy's food bowl aggression was something positive reinforcement could not have resolved. Positive reinforcement will not STOP food bowl aggression, and because a lot of trainers do not know how to use a negative consequence to stop this behavior, dogs are put to sleep. One very popular trainer (very popular in the all positive circles) tests dogs with fake hands (look up "assess a hand" on Google) and at any sign of aggression, the dog will take a one way trip to the vet's office for a lethal injection.

In fact, the very definition of positive reinforcement states you can't use it to STOP a behavior. Here is the definition of positive reinforcement:

"The offering of desirable effects or consequences for a behavior with the intention of increasing the chance of that behavior being repeated in the future."

With the intention of increasing the chance of that behavior being repeated in the future! The very definition proves you can't STOP growling, jumping, stealing, digging, pulling on leash, or any other behavior problem, and stopping behavior is what I am asked to do every day in my business.

Now on the other hand, here is the definition of positive punishment, the technical term for applying a negative consequence:

"Presenting an unfavorable outcome or event following an undesirable behavior with the goal to decrease the behavior it follows."

PUNISHMENT IS NOT ABUSE

Positive punishment is exactly what is needed to STOP behavior, still, the force-free experts will always exclusively (unsuccessfully) attempt positive reinforcement. They don't understand how to use punishment and even tell dog owners negative consequences are abusive when nothing could be further from the truth. I know dogs strike an emotional cord and the thought of an abused dog is unbearable. Heck, I can't even watch the Humane Society commercials, but punishment IS NOT abuse.

There are also a lot of trainers, like me, who have been in the game a long time. If you were training in the 1980's, there is a good chance you got your start with a choke chain, no treats, and a whole lot of force, pressure, and pain. I can see the desire to want to train with only positive reinforcement. Like many, I've seen abuse in the name of dog training first-hand. But there is a big difference between punishment and abuse, and to lump them both together is inaccurate.

Lumping punishment in with abuse is a very common tactic among big dog training organizations in this country, using it to push their flawed and dangerous ***ONLY*** positive reinforcement ideology. The Association of Pet Dog Trainers (APDT) and the Pet Professional Guild (PPG) have clear statements about the use of punishment.

From the APDT website:

"The Association of Professional Dog Trainers (APDT) supports a Least Intrusive, Minimally Aversive (LIMA) approach to behavior modification and training."

To forward their "punishment is abuse" agenda, they often make false claims of fallout and side effects including aggression. No doubt about it, abuse can absolutely make a dog aggressive, but punishment will actually help save your dog's life.

Experts keep telling dog owners any use of electronic collars is inhumane and dangerous. They say your dog will suffer side effects from using such a collar. But there are millions of dogs in this country kept safely in their yards with the use of electronic collars. Invisible Fence keeps over three million dogs safe with their pet containment systems. I would say a company like Invisible Fence has done more to save dogs' lives than all the positive only dog trainers combined. I work every day with dogs that are contained with

Invisible Fences. According to the all positive trainers, these dogs should be snarling, vicious dogs, ready to rip apart any unsuspecting person or animal that comes within a few feet of them, but we know this is simply not true. You probably personally know someone who has a very nice dog on Invisible Fence or some other type of electronic containment system in your neighborhood.

DO AS I SAY, NOT AS I DO

I do find it interesting that trainers who belong to these organizations, the enlightened ones, the tolerant, loving, never use any punishment, use positive reinforcement only people will unleash holy hell on anyone who disagrees with their dogma. The all positive, force-free crowd is against punishment for dogs but humans? Well, that's another story. They come with daggers after anyone who stands up to them and sheds light on their false doctrine.

Dog trainers who are all positive believe they have the moral high ground and can point at any trainer who uses punishment and say: "*We are better than them. We are nicer and friendlier. We use only dog-friendly training methods.*" This fancied moral high ground gives them a superior feeling. In truth, all positive dog trainers are quick to use punishment. They may not use it in dog training but with other humans, they will use punishment at the drop of a hat.

Here's a quick story for you illustrating my point. The big cheese in all positive dog training is Dr. Ian Dunbar. Dr. Dunbar, who started the Association of Pet Dog Trainers, now called the Association of Professional Dog trainers, gave a 2007 Ted Talk in Los Angeles, California.

In this talk, he discussed how we screw dogs up by using punishment and pressure. The talk gets very interesting ten minutes and thirty-one seconds in. Dr. Dunbar recalls a story of boarding a plane in Dallas, Texas and witnessing a young boy kicking the chair in front of him. The father says,

"Johnny, don't do that," but Johnny keeps kicking the chair. The father leans over and gives him ugly face. Ugly face is when you go face to face and scream at a puppy or child. Dr. Dunbar is appalled and thinks, *"Should I do something? That child has lost everything. One of the two people he can trust in this world has pulled the rug from under his feet."* Dr. Dunbar questions whether he should intervene for a second or two longer but ultimately decides to continue walking to the back of the plane. As he sits down, a thought comes to him.

This is where it gets real interesting because he goes on to say, *"If that had been a dog, I would have laid him out."*

"If that had been a dog, I would have laid him out."

I was speechless when I heard this. Here is the high priest of the Church of Positive Only Training, the Grand Poohbah and creator of the Association of Pet Dog Trainers, Dr. All Positive himself talking about assaulting a guy IF it was a puppy he gave "ugly face" to instead of a little boy, advocating physical violence to STOP the father's verbal reprimand.

I was really shocked to hear he would come to the defense of a dog and not a child, but I was also astonished he would use a negative consequence to stop the father's behavior. WHY? Why not use this as an example of how to use positive reinforcement to change the father's behavior? If science proves positive reinforcement can be used to stop bad behavior, show us how to use it to stop the man from yelling at little Johnny. Why didn't the good doctor show us how positive reinforcement can solve any problem? The Church of Positive Training is always insisting positive reinforcement can be used to change bad behavior.

He goes on, *"If he had kicked a dog, I would have punched him out."* I'm not making this up. You can find this video easily on the internet. The title is, Ian Dunbar Dog Friendly Dog Training. Why is he so quick to use violence? Why would he assault a person? And why would he step in for a dog and not a child? And why would he punch a guy? Punch a guy? That is NOT punishment. Punching someone for disagreeing is assault. Johnny's father never touched his son, he was simply scolding him and Dr. Dunbar wanted to lay him out... if it was a dog. It still baffles me.

THE REALITY IS...

Robert Ringer is one of my favorite authors. He wrote the book, *"Winning Through Intimidation,"* which has a great quote. He writes:

"Reality isn't the way you wish things to be, nor the way they appear to be, but the way they actually are."

Reality is tough for people to face. Look at the two biggest dog training organizations in this country. They can't face up to reality and instead promote dangerous dog training techniques that result in a lot of dogs getting killed every year. The methods they promote do not keep dogs safe. The best way to keep your dog safe is to have a clear understanding of how dog training works.

The reality is this... if you want to train your dog; you must apply a positive consequence to teach a behavior and a negative consequence to stop your dog from doing anything you don't like. I have stated before and it is important to clearly state again: PUNISHMENT IS NOT ABUSE.

This makes the all positive trainers squeamish and since they can't handle reality, they recommend constant management for any and all behavior problems. They would have you keep your dog in a crate or in a pen, living a life of confinement when a simple negative consequence would resolve the issue. If you do not want to keep your dog in a crate for the rest of his life, I offer you a different way to train in this book.

You may have even already hired a dog trainer to help you with some behaviors, to get your dog to listen and stop pulling, come back when called, and stop knocking over your kids. If you have, there is a good chance that trainer will provide you with a flawed training ideology which is dangerous to your dog.

Throughout this book, I will point out what you need to know and how to avoid making mistakes before departing with your hard earned money when you decide to hire a dog trainer. I will also help you learn how to train your dog. You'll discover two words every dog needs to know, how to get your dog to listen to you in distracting situations, and most importantly, how to once and for all get your dog to STOP doing undesirable behaviors. Chances are your dog is jumping, stealing, counter surfing, digging, or pulling. This book will show you how to stop any and all of these behaviors forever.

Responsibility comes with dog ownership. You are responsible for your dog twenty-four hours a day, seven days a week. Training helps keep your dog and your family safe and also makes the time you spend with your dog more enjoyable. You have a lot of choices when it comes to choosing a trainer. I encourage you to read this book with a skeptical point of view. Don't just take my word for it. Let me prove ***ONLY*** positive reinforcement training is dangerous for your dog. Let me show you using a negative consequence can save your dog's life, that negative consequences are NOT painful, mean, or abusive.

I only have one goal when I help someone train their dog. I want to give them practical, useful, effective training methods which will get the results they are looking for. There is no ideology I'm trying to promote. Everything I share is from first-hand experience, garnered from over thirty years of working professionally with thousands of people and their dogs. If it doesn't work, I don't use it.

CHAPTER 2

"Absolute faith corrupts as absolutely as absolute power."

Eric Hoffer

The True Believers From The Church Of Positive Only Training

In 1951, author Eric Hoffer wrote, *"The True Believer: Thoughts on the Nature of Mass Movements."* In 2016, the dog training profession has become a mass movement of true believers. Like most mass movements, it promotes illogical doctrines and requires a degree of faith and blind devotion.

The book is a great read and gives an understanding of human psychology and why people are drawn to mass movements. I won't give a complete book report, but I will point out how the dog training mass movement, which I call the Church of Positive Only Training, came into being and why it is dangerous for your dog. Here are the five main points of Mr. Hoffer's book and how they correlate to the world of professional dog training today.

True believers desperately need to belong.

Two of the biggest dog training organizations in the country are The Association of Professional Dog Trainers and the Pet Professional Guild. Both organizations promote an all positive dog training agenda. Together, they have thousands of members.

Mass movements always have an enemy. A mass movement does not need a God but it does need a devil.

Any dog trainer who uses or discusses using negative consequences, any trainer who does not follow the church's dogma is pointed to as the devil and threatened on social platforms.

Blind obedience is a necessary quality of a true believer.

Members of the Church of Positive Only Training will not talk out against or even discuss any disagreements with their positive only dog training agenda.

An alliance with intellectuals is important for the success of any regime.

I will show you how the Church of Positive Only Training uses the term "science-based" to promote its agenda and trick dog owners into believing a false ideology.

In the final analysis, mass movements are about change.

This is not all bad. A change was needed.

A NEEDED CHANGE

A desire to change is the catalyst for mass movements, which is not always a bad thing. The problem arises when the movement is fueled by fanaticism. This is what happened in the dog training world. The all positive dog training movement is HUGE and no one can come out and speak against it. If you are a dog trainer, you are expected to conform and follow the party line. I did for years and I'll share what happened. This all positive, force-free mass movement has been responsible for promoting a lot of false and harmful information to unsuspecting dog owners.

Reading *"The True Believer"* was eye opening. I witnessed the mass movement happening up close and personal in the profession I have worked in for over thirty years.

Eric Hoffer was a social philosopher born in 1898 in the Bronx. Concerned with the rise of Hitler and Stalin, he researched how these movements began and grew. Hoffer observed mass movements started with a desire to change. It's understandable why dog trainers wanted change.

Up until the late 1980's, dog training was often accomplished with a lot of force. Dogs performed obedience commands to avoid heavy-handed and harsh corrections. A common way to teach SIT was with a choke chain. Pressure was put on the dog's neck as the chain around it was tightened by the handler pulling up on the leash. The dog would sit to get relief from the pressure. Once in the sit position, the handler would ease up on the leash, pressure was released, and the chain was loosened. If the dog became aggressive or resisted the training, he was often hung in the air by the leash and choke collar. The leash was lifted with force and the dog's front paws would come off the ground. The more the dog resisted, the harsher the leash corrections became.

It was and still is a very brutal way to train. If you've observed it, and I have, you can see the dog go into survival mode. He thinks he may die and will often do everything he can to get away from the trainer. The old school trainers take this as the dog resisting their commands and increase the correction. The dog will panic and it is awful to witness. The trainer will defend his actions and say he had to correct the dog. Some of the trainers I observed were brutal.

There absolutely needed to be a change, so when positive reinforcement was introduced, it immediately became popular with many dog trainers looking for a more humane way to work with dogs. Within a few years, a mass movement was started and the leaders of it decided any negative consequence at all was tantamount to abuse.

A few prominent trainers came on the scene in the mid 1980's and started demonstrating positive reinforcement techniques. Clicker training gained popularity in the early 1990's and became widespread due to seminars given by Gary Wilkes and Karen Pryor. Dr. Ian Dunbar's Sirius Puppy Training Program caught on with many trainers and then in 1993, with the founding of the Association of Pet Dog Trainers (now the Association of Professional Dog Trainers) by Dr. Dunbar, the mass movement was launched. With the formation of APDT, legions of dog trainers became fanatical about using ONLY positive reinforcement. As fanatics do, they labeled anyone who disagreed with them as an outdated, unscientific, and ABUSIVE dog trainer.

What started as change in a positive direction, over time, morphed into what I like to call the Church of Positive Only Training because the dog trainers who belong behave like zealots. The church has its members, priests, and priestesses. The congregation floods the internet, magazines, and TV shows, pushing a flawed ideology that has gone so far over the top, it no longer helps dogs. In fact, it is downright dangerous for dogs.

THE NEED TO BELONG

Power is often found in large numbers. In his book, Mr. Hoffer writes true believers desperately need to belong. Since the early nineties, groups for dog trainers have been forming and two have emerged as the largest dog training organizations on the planet. The Association of Pet Dog Trainers (APDT) mentioned earlier was formed in 1993 and in 2012; The Pet Professional Guild (PPG) was formed.

The PPG felt APDT was not positive or force-free enough and members signed up in droves. PPG is big with being "force-free" and I would say is even more radical than APDT. PPG has grown at a rapid pace and shows Mr. Hoffer was correct, church members desperately need to belong. Belonging to a group gives church members a feeling of superiority because they have large organizations backing them up. Because of their numbers and certification programs, church members become very arrogant and try to bully non-members. You may think I am exaggerating but comments on my YouTube videos prove otherwise. I also know comments on Amazon will be scathing because of what I am writing.

THE COMMON ENEMY

Enemies are the fastest way for a movement to gain momentum. Without an enemy there is no "fire in the belly." To start a mass movement you need to be able to point to someone or something and proclaim it is the devil. Being able to point to a common enemy is the fastest way to gain trust among members. Church members are quickly identified and then band together against evil dog trainers. The Church of Positive Only Training has pointed to any dog trainer using negative consequences as the devil. Those trainers are labeled as uneducated, abusive, unscientific, and mean.

Church members think they have the moral high ground and hit the streets running, letting everyone know who the devil is, namely being any dog trainer who would dare use a choke, prong, or electronic collar. Any dog trainer who still refers to dominance theory is a hack and must be eradicated. Again, do a quick Google search and take a look at what you see. The church has become very powerful by pointing out the devil and many "experts" and reality TV stars have followed suit. They have joined the choir because they do not want to be labeled as abusive. That would be bad for business.

BLIND OBEDIENCE

As Mr. Hoffer wrote, "*The blindness of the fanatic is a source of strength (he sees no obstacles), but it is the cause of intellectual sterility and emotional monotony. The fanatic is also mentally cocky, and hence barren of new beginnings. At the root of his cockiness is the conviction of life and the universe conforming to a simple formula - his formula. His is thus without the fruitful intervals of groping, when the mind is as it were in solution - ready for all manner of new reactions, new combinations and new beginnings.*"

Blind obedience is a necessity. The high priests of the Church of Positive Only Training come out with training statements and they are followed as gospel. No questions asked, no thought involved, they are just regurgitated as favorite little sayings that back their false notions. Here's a favorite quote by Dr. Ian Dunbar:

"To use shock as an effective dog training method you will need: A thorough understanding of canine behavior. A thorough understanding of learning theory. Impeccable timing. And if you have those three things, you don't need a shock collar."

Church members LOVE this quote even though it makes no sense. To prove my point, let's go back to Invisible Fence. For it to work, and this is fact not opinion, you don't need to know anything about canine behavior, you don't need to know anything about learning theory, and you could be a card carrying member of Tardy Anonymous and the system will still keep your dog in the yard. What I just wrote is absolute fact! There are millions of dogs all over the United States debunking Dr. Dunbar's oft quoted statement on shock collars. But it doesn't matter to church members. They take this quote and repeat it over and over. No thinking takes place. Let a member of the Church of Positive Only Training read the last few paragraphs and they will attack you.

And here's the funny part. Let's say I understand canine behavior better than anyone on the planet. I act like a dog because I understand it so well. If you were to come visit me I would sniff your butt instead of shake your hand because I understand canine behavior so well. For learning theory, I have channeled the spirits of Ivan Pavlov and BF Skinner. There is no one in the universe who understands classical and operant conditioning as thoroughly as I do. My timing is better than the Karate Kid with chopsticks. I can catch TWO flies because my timing is that good.

So now I want to keep my dog in the yard. There is no need to use a shock collar because I am so awesome at using positive reinforcement. I use all my knowledge as an expert on canine behavior; I know learning theory and have impeccable timing. I offer my dog the best, most high-value treat based on this knowledge. I am going to teach my dog to stay in the yard. With my thorough understanding of canine behavior, my complete understanding of learning theory, and my impeccable timing I'll be able to teach my dog to stay in the yard. Here comes a squirrel. I pull out my high value reward using my thorough understanding of canine behavior. I give my dog a cue using my skills as someone who knows learning theory, my timing is perfect and my dog... runs after the squirrel and leaves the yard.

What happened? Simple, you can't use all that understanding of canine behavior, learning theory, and timing to STOP behavior, but blind obedience will continue to perpetuate the myth.

There is a condition the Church of Positive Only Training members suffer from. It is called cognitive dissonance. Cognitive dissonance is the discomfort experienced by a person who holds onto a belief and is then confronted with information which conflicts with their existing beliefs, ideas, or values. The individual becomes psychologically uncomfortable. I've seen it first-hand. The person will try to reduce the dissonance and in the case of church members, they will attack non-believers.

Another explanation I've seen is this:

"Sometimes people hold a core belief that is very strong. When they are presented with evidence that works against that belief, the new evidence cannot be accepted. It would create a feeling that is extremely uncomfortable, called cognitive dissonance. And because it is so important to protect the core belief, they will rationalize, ignore and even deny anything that doesn't fit in with the core belief."

In 1957, social psychologist, Leon Festinger, wrote the book, *A Theory of Cognitive Dissonance.* Festinger uses smoking as an example. Everyone knows smoking is bad for your health. Smoke for a few years and your body will feel it. You'll get winded going up stairs, you'll cough more, get sick frequently, have wrinkly skin, stained teeth, etc. But for the person who loves smoking, he deals with his dissonance by justifying what he does. Even though he knows it is bad for his health, he will mentally minimize the risks of smoking. A common statement by a committed smoker is, *"MY Aunt Martha smoked four packs of cigarettes every day for seventy years. She started smoking at six and lived to ninety-nine."* Smokers decide smoking is more important than their health. Cigarettes have more value than their health.

Punishment has been built up for so long as being abusive, as having terrible side effects, as a course of action which can never be used, the all positive dog trainer will have the dog die before recommending the use of punishment. So my question is always the same. Would you use punishment to save a dog's life? I would and do every day. I am much more interested in saving dogs' lives than sticking to a flawed, ineffective ideology.

INTELLECTUAL ALLIANCE

For the mass movement to grow the way it has, church members have strongly aligned themselves with "science based" training methods. Or as Mr. Hoffer wrote:

"The man of words relentlessly attempts to "discredit the prevailing creeds" and creates a "hunger for faith" which is then fed by "doctrines and slogans of the new faith."

"Science based dog training" is the cornerstone for all of the members' arguments. You can't argue with science based dog training unless you are a dolt and an idiot. Church members constantly associate themselves with intellectuals to try and control the conversation. It has helped them gain huge numbers for their organizations and convince dog owners the only way to train is by following their methods and techniques because after all, they're science based.

The high priestess of dog training, Victoria Stilwell, can be observed on YouTube. In church member fashion, she actually proclaims herself the God of dog training. Think I'm kidding? You can see the video on my website, DeadlyDogTrainingMyth.com. In this video, Victoria and two other judges, Allan Reznik and Wendy Diamond, are critiquing a group of dog trainers. Wendy Diamond gives high marks to a trainer for his performance. Stilwell is beside herself and can't wait to speak up.

Stilwell, *"I have to step in there. Because I believe that any trainer or owner who uses dominance and submission methodology, THAT'S MEDIEVAL DOG TRAINING! The best scientists, ethologists, and behaviorists in this country agree that to train your dog in a positive manner gives the dog confidence and security."*

Wendy speaks up and tells Victoria she has her way and he has his way. Victoria is angry and disagrees with her. Wendy adds everyone has their own way of training. Victoria, spoken like a true church member, pipes in and keeps trying to prove her point by stating she has "science" on her side. As I've mentioned, this is a classic church member move. Wendy throws her hand up and says, *"You're the God of dog training?"* Stilwell yells, *"YES, because I follow the very best in this country."* Wendy states: *"This is just ridiculous."*

This is the point that illustrates Victoria as a fanatic of the mass movement. She loses it and smacks her hand down and yells she is not ridiculous. She also states she is also going to get very angry with Wendy. Angry? Why doesn't she use positive reinforcement to make her point?

It's interesting to watch because I have been face to face with True Believers and if they are a new convert, watch out. The best course of action is to move on because you are dealing with someone who is operating on solely on emotion. All logic has left the room.

The most important part of this angry exchange between Victoria and Wendy is when she claims she has science on her side. Remember, Eric Hoffer wrote, *"An alliance with intellectuals is important for any successful regime or Mass Movement."* Since the Church of Positive Only Training's inception, the True Believer congregation has always promoted the notion it has science backing it up. This is essential to keep the church growing.

Here is the statement from the homepage of the Pet Professional Guild website (petprofessionalguild.com):

"The Pet Professional Guild is a membership organization representing pet industry professionals who are committed to results based; science based force-free training and pet care. Pet Professional Guild members understand force-free to mean: No Shock, No Pain, No Choke, No Fear, No Physical Force, No Compulsion Based Methods are employed to train or care for a pet. Join PPG today and help us educate and engage more pet professionals and pet owners. Become a steward of the science based, results based force-free message, philosophy and training practices."

And from the Association of Professional Dog Trainers, How to Choose a Dog Trainer webpage (apdt.com/pet-owners/choosing-a-trainer):

"Because APDT is primarily an educational organization for trainers, we allow trainers with all methodologies to join with the goal of exposing them to humane, science-based training methods."

And from the APDT Fact Sheet page (apdt.com/docs/apdt/apdt-fact-sheet.pdf):

"Membership in the Association is open to all who pay annual dues and includes individuals with a wide range of experience, knowledge, and skills. The APDT is primarily an educational organization and promotes using positive, science-based methods that focus on rewarding behaviors and eschews training based on physical punishment and intimidation."

The problem is there is nothing science based with much of what they preach. What they are really doing is following an ideology and pushing a flawed training theory which does not help the dog ever get the correct information. An all positive training theory sets the dog up for failure.

Consequences are nothing more than information to your dog. Dogs need both negative and positive consequences to figure out their surroundings. A dog has to learn to live like a human and without the correct information, the dog is setup to fail. It really is sad the all positive crowd cannot figure this out as more and more dogs end up going to shelters or are killed because they were never given the correct information.

Church members will still insist positive reinforcement is the only way to train. If your dog is jumping, biting, or stealing the pizza off the table, use positive reinforcement. Punishment is to be avoided at all costs. But according to the scientific definition of positive reinforcement, *it is the offering of desirable effects or consequences for a behavior with the intention of* ***increasing*** *the chance of that behavior being repeated in the future.*

This is where it gets fun with church members. This is the correct, scientific definition so how can positive reinforcement be used to stop your dog from stealing food off the counter? How are you going to use treats or praise to stop this behavior?

YOU CAN'T!

Now here is the scientific definition of punishment:

The goal of punishment is to decrease the behavior that it follows. In the case of positive punishment, it involves presenting an unfavorable outcome or event following an undesirable behavior.

If you want your dog to STOP stealing food off the counter, to STOP jumping, to STOP digging, to STOP biting, or to STOP any other behavior, you must use punishment. And let me again state for the record: Punishment is NOT abuse.

Church members at this point will argue punishment does not teach the dog what to do, which is completely ridiculous. Of course it doesn't teach the dog what to do. That is NOT how punishment works. Punishment does not increase behavior. It decreases or eliminates behavior.

Punishment can save your dog's life. Not to beat a dead horse, but millions of dogs are safe in their yards with underground electronic containment systems. This is accomplished by the use of punishment, NOT positive reinforcement. If you tried using ONLY positive reinforcement to keep your dog in the yard, there is a good chance your dog will end up dead. This is not opinion, it is not following an ideology, it is science. Without a physical barrier, the best way to keep your dog safe in the yard is through the use of punishment. If it could be accomplished with treats there would be a huge business associated with it. There would be a Positive Reinforcement Containment System. But there isn't. Why? BECAUSE TREATS WILL NOT STOP YOUR DOG FROM LEAVING THE YARD.

Positive reinforcement can't stop behaviors. If you want to stop your dog from leaving the yard, you'll have to apply punishment. You must use punishment for crossing a boundary. THIS IS SCIENCE! In order to counter this, the church members lament an underground containment system will have lifelong negative side effects on the dog. The dog will develop aggression, become fearful, and display other unwanted behaviors. Look around. Do you know anyone with a dog on Invisible Fence? Where I live in Southeastern Massachusetts there are thousands of dogs using this containment system. They live a happy life with their human families without the dreaded side effects the church proclaims.

You'd think faced with this factual, scientific information a church member would concede and agree punishment, a negative consequence, is the way you stop behavior. But humans are emotional animals, and once a person is thinking with emotion, logic has no place at the table. Instead, a church member will change gears and bring out the big dogs. They will quote the Veterinary Society of Animal Behavior. This group should know how behavior works; they will clear it all up. Here is their position on punishment:

"AVSAB recommends that training should focus on reinforcing desired behaviors, removing the reinforcer for inappropriate behaviors, and addressing the emotional state and environmental conditions driving the undesirable behavior. This approach promotes a better understanding of the pet's behavior and better awareness of how humans may have inadvertently contributed to the development of the undesirable behavior."

Wait a minute. You guys are the experts. You're the American Veterinary Society of Animal Behavior! Which desired behavior should I reinforce when my dog is stealing food off the counter? Which behavior do I reinforce to keep my dog in the yard when a squirrel runs by? What's the underlying reason for the dog leaving the yard? He chases squirrels. Do I get rid of all the squirrels and he'll stay in the yard? Did I inadvertently teach my dog to steal food off the counter? So it's my fault my dog does behaviors I don't like? I get it. I taught my dog to knock over the trash, to grab the toilet paper and destroy it into a million pieces. Thank you American Veterinary Society of Animal Behavior for pointing out my dog's bad behavior is my fault.

Crazy, right?

This is the EXACT reason why I named this book, *The Deadly Dog Training Myth*. The experts won't give it to you straight. Do what they say and your dog will never get trained. They follow a flawed ideology and push an all positive agenda that will not get you the results you want and need. The experts tell you positive reinforcement is necessary to stop unwanted behaviors. Or they will tell you to redirect the behavior, counter-condition, desensitize and use other absurd methods when all that is required is a simple negative consequence.

Let me share a little secret with you. The American Veterinary Society of Animal Behavior is part of the church. They are the intellectuals behind behavior and every dog trainer is supposed to bow down and concede they are the authority. Like Mr. Hoffer wrote:

"It's disconcerting to realize that businessmen, generals, soldiers, men of action are less corrupted by power than intellectuals... You take a conventional man of action, and he's satisfied if you obey. But not the intellectual. He doesn't want you just to obey. He wants you to get down on your knees and praise the one who makes you love what you hate and hate what you love. In other words, whenever the intellectuals are in power, there's soul-raping going on."

MY OWN EXPERIENCE WITH THE MASS MOVEMENT

I can speak the way I do about the Church of Positive Only Training because I know it well. Depressed is one word I could use to describe my state of mind back in 2006. By then, I had been a card carrying member of the church for eleven years and attended six APDT conferences. I had been working professionally with dogs since 1985 and still did not like the results I was getting. I had gone and studied the experts up close. I wholeheartedly bought into the notion when I could not get the results my clients needed with all positive training it must have been me. I became so depressed by the whole situation I dropped out of dog training. I sold my business and decided to go into another field. I kept a few websites up and running but I was no longer personally working with clients helping them train their dogs.

After a good seven to eight years out of the game and some serious soul searching, I woke up one day with the realization I still wanted to help people with their dogs, and when I dove back in, I realized the church had been wrong all along with much of what they were preaching.

You see, complicated training methods allow the church to get away with poor results. Along with asserting they are doing "science based" dog training at anyone who challenges them, it is easy to blame the trainer or dog owner for not doing it right. I stayed a member of the church for a long time because I had seen the dark side of dog training up close. I had seen dogs abused in the name of training. I was a ready and willing convert. Positive reinforcement training sounded great. Thinking I could do everything using ONLY positive reinforcement, I jumped in with both feet and learned all I could. No one was more excited than me when I found the church.

As I look back now, I see clearly they wanted you to believe if you did not get the results they claimed, it wasn't the technique it was you. So when your dog kept jumping and knocking the kids over, it was your fault. They have at their disposal loads of different complex training protocols which will make you dizzy just looking at them. Desensitization and counterconditioning are two of their big favorites. The church has developed and promotes these complicated and next to useless training programs. Some of these protocols have as many as fifty steps to complete over a month's time. When the training fails, it is not the positive only trainer, protocol, or the dog that is at fault. Instead, the blame is placed squarely on the shoulders of the owner for not following the instructions correctly.

Church members' core beliefs are so strong about punishment they will have their clients spend weeks, months, and even years following these complicated procedures. When someone like me steps forward and recommends punishment to solve the problem in a single training session it makes church members want to rip their hair out.

When punishment is used in the correct way, it takes a split second of putting the dog in a little discomfort. Remember, a negative consequence is information. Punishment is NOT abuse. It is information to help the dog learn what is not acceptable behavior.

The sad part is church members are so opposed to using or recommending punishment, dogs often die. Church members would rather the dog be euthanized than be momentarily placed in slight discomfort. I know this is a strong statement but it is very true.

A dog with a jumping problem can very easily end up in a shelter and be put to sleep. I can help you fix your dog's jumping problem in less than ten minutes to avoid that very outcome. Once you understand how to use punishment the correct way, you can now give your dog the information he needs to live in your house. If you want your dog to stop jumping, punishment is how you will accomplish it. Church members will have you ignore, redirect, and spend months rewarding for not jumping. They will in unison state: *"Teach your dog what you want him to do,"* and when you follow that advice, you will still have a jumping dog. However, jumping will stop the day you apply punishment. You can get it done and over with, never to return, in ten minutes or less, and if you suffer with this behavior, don't worry, I'll show you exactly how to stop it later in the book.

Good things do come from mass movements though. There is a lot of good which came out of the change that took place back in the early 90's, but the church has evolved and the agenda is now dangerous. Even though many changes have been for the good, it has gone way too far and the whole force-free training push is not helping dogs.

As good as it may sound to some, there is no such thing as force-free. People get so wrapped up in these movements they become ridiculous. What I see now in the movement is amazing. They are all trying to "out positive" each other. Who can be the most positive? Gentle leaders, a great tool for helping dogs walk on leash, are now considered too harsh by the force-free crowd. Camps are created for dogs to experience a stress free week with their owner. Some are even abandoning the whole idea of training and are saying all problems can be solved with love. The move towards more positive training methods was good but it is now becoming absurd. Pretty soon the all positive crowd will want to give dogs voting rights.

And here's something to think about that puts this whole notion of force-free into perspective. My best friend, a groomer, can rip hair out of your dog's ears or cause fear and possibly pain while clipping his nails. Vets can remove or alter your dog's reproductive system which will cause pain for days. Veterinarians, groomers, and anyone else in the pet industry routinely cause your dog pain, fear, and discomfort and nobody bats an eye. If pain and fear are applied in the name of health, you can do it all you want.

But if I do it in the name of behavior, I am labeled abusive. What I do as a dog trainer, when applying a lifesaving negative consequence, is much gentler and is over almost instantly, but the church has decided no negative consequence, no punishment is to ever be used because it will damage the dog. According to them, the dog will suffer the side effects for the rest of his life. What about all the other fearful experiences the dog is exposed to? Why do they get a free pass? Are you starting to see the absurdity of all of this?

And here is the response from the all positive, force-free trainers:

WE HAVE SCIENCE TO BACK US UP! WE ARE RIGHT AND YOU ARE WRONG BECAUSE SCIENCE SAYS SO.

Well, science is a subjective and fickle beast.

CHAPTER 3

"Get your facts first, and then you can distort them as much as you please."

Mark Twain

Smelling Farts May Prevent Cancer

Why Listening To The "Science-Based" Dog Trainers Can Get Your Dog Killed

"Back off man, I'm a scientist."
Peter Venkman from the movie, Ghostbusters

That's a great scene because it's true. I'm a scientist so you have no right to question me even though science is so subjective. Pull out the science card and everyone is supposed to back off and debate or conversation is over. So how can a guy with no college education, a guy who graduated high school at the very bottom of his class, a guy with learning disabilities say science is a load of crap? Keep reading...

The title of this chapter may disgust some of you but before you start sending me hate mail, please get upset with Time Magazine first and their July 11, 2014 issue. Offensive is the first word my wife used when she saw the title of this chapter. *"Don't blame me,"* I said. If she didn't like the name of the chapter she could contact Time and let them know. This is the actual title of an article which appeared in their July 11, 2014 issue. I chose this title because science is very subjective. There is so much BS surrounding scientific studies it is mind boggling why anyone would even point to science anymore to back up a claim.

Science has become so subjective because studies conducted today are funded by people with a vested interest in a certain outcome. If scientists want to keep the research money coming in, they need to be sure the scientific studies arrive at certain results. Scientists at universities have tremendous pressure to provide information which helps the client.

Did you know there is even a term for getting the desired results during scientific studies? It is called P-hacking, also known as data-dredging, snooping, fishing, significance-chasing, and double dipping. University of Pennsylvania psychologist, Uri Simonsohn, and his colleagues came up with the term P-hacking. *"P-hacking,"* says Simonsohn, *"is trying multiple things until you get the desired result - even unconsciously."* False and manipulating information is always being pushed on the public in the name of science.

Look at the tobacco companies. For years they said, *"Science can't prove smoking is bad for your health."* Tobacco companies didn't say, *"YOU can't prove smoking is bad for you."* Instead they said, *"SCIENCE can't prove smoking is bad for you."*

Each individual will develop their own set of beliefs based on their personal experiences. Take the very emotional issue of global warming. Listen to each side of the political aisle. You can spend five minutes researching and you'll discover science proves global warming is real AND fake. There are pages and pages of scientific data backing up both sides. Before you hit the ceiling and think I am supporting one side over the other, I'm only pointing out anyone can find information to back up his stance on a subject.

Recently, NBC's Today Show, which loves scientific studies, had Al Roker, Natalie Morales, and Tamron Hall discussing the health benefits of whole milk. There were scientific studies about whether it was or was not healthy for you. Al Roker jumped in and said, "*You find the study that sounds best to you and go with that.*" This is NOT how science works, but it's what everyone is doing, especially the all positive, force-free crowd. For years, they have been claiming to have science on their side when it isn't.

YOU CAN FIND A STUDY FOR ANYTHING

Not only do you have scientific studies with rigged outcomes, you also have scientific studies which border on the ridiculous and generate insane headlines. This is the reason you have a Time Magazine article proclaiming you can cure cancer by smelling farts.

Here are some examples of actual scientific studies:

- **Late night snacking affects brain**, led by a team at the University of California, Los Angeles
- **Pizza is the most addictive food**, conducted by the students at the University of Michigan
- **Hugging your dog is bad for your dog**, conducted by Dr. Stanley Coren, Ph. D., F.R.S.C.
- **Driving while dehydrated is just as dangerous as driving drunk**, led by Professor Ron Maughan, Emeritus Professor of Sport and Exercise Nutrition, at Loughborough University

- **Drinking wine is better than going to the gym**, conducted at Canada's University of Alberta

I love that last one!

This is from winerist.com:

"It's long been thought that red wine possesses many positive health benefits, but today, wine lovers, your dreams are going to be answered. A new scientific study has shown that, on top of all the other reported benefits, a glass of wine a day can be more beneficial for you than an hour at the gym! Yes, you read that right... there's scientific proof that red wine is better than the gym!"

Imagine if you sell wine or gym memberships. Don't go to the gym, just crack open your favorite bottle of Merlot and slurp away. Forget grunting and sweating, you can just guzzle some fermented grape juice and you'll get better results than an hour spent at the gym. And if you don't believe me... we have *SCIENTIFIC PROOF* red wine is better than Planet Fitness!

From The Huffington Post:

"Dear red wine drinkers: I have wonderful news. A new study says that drinking a glass of wine can equate to an hour of exercise. I repeat: Drinking a glass of freaking merlot could be just as good for you as an hour of working out at the gym. Feel free to commence rejoicing at this time.

The researchers responsible for the glorious study — which was published in the Journal of Physiology in May — discovered that resveratrol, a "natural compound" found in certain fruits, nuts, and (you guessed it) red wine, could actually "enhance exercise training and performance." But there's more. Jason Dyck, the principal investigator for the study, tells Science Daily that resveratrol can also offer the same benefits working out does."

From Science Daily:

"We were excited when we saw that resveratrol showed results similar to what you would see from extensive endurance exercise training," says Dyck, who works in the Faculty of Medicine & Dentistry as a researcher in the department of Pediatrics and the department of Pharmacology. "We immediately saw the potential for this and thought that we identified improved exercise performance in a pill."

Principal investigator, Jason Dyck, and his team's findings were published in the peer-reviewed *Journal of Physiology* in late May 2012.

Armed with all this scientific research, no one can question your authority. You can point to Science Daily and researcher Jason Dyck, and be assured drinking a glass of wine is all you need. No more expensive gym memberships. If anyone gives you any lip, you can tell them that the findings were published in the peer-reviewed Journal of Physiology.

Or you could just say, *"Back off man. I'm a scientist! I have scientific proof on my side, what do you have? Common sense? Actual results? Logic? None of that matters... I have science!"*

To get the true story requires a little digging. In an interview with CBC.ca, when asked about, *"A glass of red wine being equivalent to an hour at the gym,"* researcher Jason Dyck said, *"No, sadly that's not the case, although I think many people want to believe that."*

KEY POINT: MANY PEOPLE WANT TO BELIEVE.

What the study did find was resveratrol, a compound found in grapes, can increase the capacity for those already exercising. *"We didn't use any red wine in our study nor did we recommend not going to the gym,"* said Dyck. The study did conclude resveratrol could help people on restricted exercise programs. *"The concentration of resveratrol as a performance enhancing sup-*

plement would have to be so concentrated you'd have to drink between one hundred to one thousand bottles of wine a day," Dyck added.

Wait a minute! The headlines stated, *"Science Proves Wine Is Better Than An Hour In The Gym!"* But it's not the truth by a longshot. This and smelling farts to cure cancer were used as examples. When "experts" assert they have science backing them up, you should raise a skeptical eye... especially when it comes to dog trainers!

I BOUGHT IN

I fell for it too. Science was what attracted me to the all positive philosophy. As a dog trainer who had been exposed to very harsh training methods, I was hungry to learn a better and more sophisticated way to train dogs. When positive reinforcement, science-based dog training came on my radar, I was hooked. There were so many seminars, books, associations, and speakers to learn from. I ate it up like a hot fudge sundae with Ben and Jerry's ice cream. I traveled the country to learn as much as I could from the science-based experts. After a few years of attending conferences and seminars, I was disappointed to see the same speakers telling the same stories over and over, with little to zero actual results.

I realized intellectuals don't care about results as much as they care about their position, no matter what it is. Dog trainers who push science-based training methods using positive reinforcement feel they are superior and have the moral high ground. They use it to point to any trainer who uses punishment and pressure and accuse, *"That dog trainer is outdated and abusive."* Remember our friend, Victoria Stilwell? She called the trainer MEDIEVAL.

As I continued along the all positive dog training path, I realized the church members always had an ace in the hole. They would always blame the owner if their methods couldn't fix the problem. So if you had a dog who barked his head off, the all positive trainer would have you carrying out all sorts of gyrations to get your dog to stop barking. He would have you do puppy pushups, put the barking on cue, find out what the underlying problem was, exercise your dog for hours a day, teach nose work, and a whole host of other useless time wasting techniques when it comes to actually fixing the problem. If a dog is barking incessantly, you can stop it within a few minutes if you know how to use punishment. Cue the science crowd shrieking in horror at reading this.

My wife, Rachael, adopted a yellow lab years ago that had been a repeat visitor to the local shelter. If he went back once more, he wasn't coming out. She was this dog's last chance. Owen was a handsome boy and was pretty well-mannered but he would not stop barking. He went on long hikes, swam at the beach, played ball for hours, but would still not stop barking. Owen would literally lie on the living room floor, completely wiped out, almost nodding off to sleep, and bark. Rachael went to different trainers and was given the typical, all positive advice which did nothing to help her or the dog. You see, barking is often the result of overstimulation. The dog can't help himself and will bark and bark, even when exercised to the point of exhaustion. When the appropriate punishment is applied, the dog will calm down.

To combat my advice (which is the correct advice by the way) all positive dog trainers insist the dog will suffer horrific side effects from the applied punishment. They will howl together as one voice crying out using punishment will lead to fear and aggression. The all positive crowd always uses this as a backup when faced with someone like me who disagrees with them.

But none of that is true. It is "fake science" because no one really studies punishment. And since they never actually use punishment to have any credible first-hand experience, they repeat what they've been told over and over for years. Remember, punishment is NOT abuse. Used correctly, it is an effective way to communicate life-saving information to your dog. And in Owen's case, I can say with absolute certainty it saved his life and he never showed any signs of aggression in his remaining twelve plus years.

ANECDOTAL EVIDENCE

I can hear it now. Well Mr. Smarty Pants, what makes you so right? Why should I listen to you? The big difference between church members and me is I want people to do what they think is right. If after reading my book you disagree with me, no problem. That's not the way the church works though. You agree, or else!

I know many people get uneasy around the topic of punishment. I worked with a very nice couple that had a high energy lab puppy. This puppy was jumping, biting, and ripping the woman's clothes. When I suggested punishment to stop the behavior, she was clearly uncomfortable. I told her she did not have to do anything she did not want to; she could manage the pup's behavior with a crate and leash. I added if she ever changed her mind to let me know. Three ripped shirts later she called. I showed her how to use punishment to stop the behavior and she no longer needed to make a weekly stop at Macy's. Needless to say, she was happy with the results.

Even so, you may still be skeptical. That is good. Don't take my word for it. I just want to help you train your dog. I want you to get results so I provide the most practical advice I can. I never rely on anecdotal evidence, unlike the entire congregation of the Church of Positive Only Training. Most of what they preach relies heavily on anecdotal evidence and they all regurgitate it back blindly, claiming to be science-based, which is kind of funny because anecdotal evidence is about as unscientific as you can get. You see, anecdotal evidence is based on hearsay rather than hard facts, these are stories people share that are based on very limited, cherry-picked examples they have usually heard from someone else to imply a generalization. The all positive crowd has heard using any type of negative consequence or punishment results in lifelong, irrefutable damage and the dog will never be able to recover from the fall out of the punishment. One popular all positive dog trainer, Steve White, loves to say this:

"Punishment is like a nuclear bomb. If the blast doesn't get you the fallout will."

Really? Again, punishment is NOT abuse. Abuse will have long term effects but punishment is information. Most of us fall off our bikes when we first learn how to ride. It can be painful, even scary, but it doesn't stop us from getting back on the seat and pedaling down the road. Falling off the bike provides information you need to learn how to ride your bike in a safe manner. Any fallout is information stored in your melon to use at a later date to keep you safe while riding around on your Huffy.

GO AHEAD AND THANK B.F. SKINNER

So where did all this very unscientific, science-based training theory come from? The scientist that started it all was Burrhus Frederic Skinner, born in Susquehanna, Pennsylvania in 1904. He was an American psychologist and author and is often viewed as THE big cheese of behavior and operant conditioning. After hanging around Greenwich Village for a year trying to write the next great American novel, ole B.F. decided to hang it up on writing and became interested in behavior. He was accepted into Harvard University and studied psychology, receiving his PH.D in 1931. When it comes to science and behavior, it all stops when B.F. Skinner's name is thrown into the mix.

As a tenured professor at Harvard, author of twenty-one books and one hundred eighty articles, inventor of the Skinner box and the Air Crib for babies, you had better back off when that kind of firepower is used. But... if we really want to get to the heart of the matter, if we really want to understand where the confusion with behavior starts, I would point to the supreme egghead himself. The great B.F. Skinner is at the very beginning of the all positive movement. He is the one who started the whole mess because as a scientist, who should have been an unemotional observer, he let his feelings get in the way.

You see, Skinner did not like punishment so he suggested punishment was an ineffective way to control behavior. He believed punishment only led to short term behavior changes and using punishment on the subject (dog) would result in the subject (dog) attempting to avoid the punisher. Since punishment was not liked by the Godfather of Behavior, it was linked to side effects. Punishment was associated with fallout, labeled as ineffective, and therefore, it was not recommended as the best course of action.

So the roots of the Church of Positive Only Training started with B.F. Skinner. The members latched on like a tick to a big dog. Then our old friend, anecdotal evidence, came into play and was used to push the anti-punishment, all positive, force-free movement. If you were to ask me, I would say Uncle B.F. was the granddaddy of anecdotal evidence. He was the one whose personal feelings about behavior were more important than actual data and so he pushed an ideology which caught on like wildfire with the church members.

THE CHURCH'S FIVE MAIN TENETS

Every church has its tenets and The Church of Positive Only has theirs. They teach, share, and follow these statements as gospel. Some very popular ones they include with their (pseudo) science-based training theory are:

Tenet #1: The behavior may return when punishment stops.

Reapplication is totally fine when you are handing treats to a dog, but if you must reapply punishment, it is a sin to church members. You can reward the sit command over, and over, and over, but reapplying punishment is not acceptable. A dog will learn much faster from properly applied punishment than from all the treats in the world.

My mother installed Invisible Fence for her little cairn terrier over fifteen years ago. Some of her friends told her the system wouldn't work for terriers because they are too tough and strong willed. I remember helping with the training. Her little terrier, Spunky, received three corrections from the fence. Spunky is still alive at the time of this writing. My parents live in a house on the water and everyone loves being outside there. Spunky has not had to have the punishment reapplied in years. In fact, after the three corrections she never received another one. If the dog is constantly being punished for the same behavior, the trainer needs to re-evaluate the punishment because the right information isn't being communicated. Sometimes the behavior may need a reminder, but it is no different than giving a dog another treat to keep a desired behavior strong.

Tenet #2: Punishment only suppresses behaviors, it doesn't change the underlying cause.

Suppression of undesired behaviors is what you want. When you punish a behavior your goal is to reduce or eliminate the behavior. Any talk of suppression makes the church members go wild. They believe suppression of the behavior will sink deep down into the dog's psyche and fester. As the behavior is suppressed it is building and just waiting for a chance to resurface. Except when it does resurface it will be in the form of an out of control, snarling, fang-toothed dog bent on hell and destruction. They are mixing up repressed feelings with suppressed behavior.

A behavior which is punished will go away if the punishment is applied correctly and there will be no side effects if the dog is then taught what behavior is desired. You can completely stop a dog from crossing a boundary, stealing garbage, counter surfing, or jumping with suppression. I can cure most dogs of jumping in five minutes. Once the behavior is suppressed, it will not resurface and create a dog that will tear apart anyone who crosses his path. The jumping is stopped through punishment and then the dog is only rewarded for keeping his paws on the ground.

Tenet #3: Punishment is rewarding to the punisher.

Ridiculous and absurd is all I can say about this lovely little tenet. I have never taken on a new client and evilly rubbed my hands together and thought, *"Oh boy, a new dog to punish. Using all this punishment is like crack, it just makes me want to do it more and now I have a new subject to use it on, hahahaha!"*

The idea of using punishment because it is reinforcing to me (the punisher) is beyond insane. Ninety-eight percent of the training I do with a dog is positive. I use verbal markers and always spend the first few sessions talking about rewards and reinforcing behaviors, but the all positive trainers will point to anyone who uses negative consequences and label him a crack addicted, punishment junkie. I came across a post on Facebook from a trainer who wrote, *"Humans learn to love using punishment because it is so reinforcing."*

I DON'T love using punishment, but I do LOVE the results punishment can give me in a training situation because I LOVE dogs and know punishment can save a dog's life. Oh boy, can I see that statement being distorted and not quoted correctly.

This is the kind of ridiculousness that is pushed on dog owners by the Church of Positive Only Training. There is nothing rewarding about punishing a dog. It is rewarding to see a dog stay in the yard and know he is safe. It is rewarding to stop a dog from jumping when you know he is out of that house if the behavior doesn't end. It is rewarding to see a dog do a rocket fast recall command, or to watch a dog learn to hold a dumbbell in his mouth through the use of positive reinforcement. But instead, church members point to the enemy and say, *"Punishment is rewarding for the punisher! They are a bunch of punishment addicted, outdated, medieval dog trainers. They get excited about punishing dogs and we are better than them."*

Tenet #4: Punishment can damage the dog's confidence, trust in the trainer, and relationship between dog and human.

Believe it or not, using a negative consequence for unacceptable behavior will actually improve the relationship. One good negative consequence can calm a dog down and completely change the relationship for the better. When I am called in to help, many times it's because the dog can't control himself anymore. The dog overstimulates and continues to ramp up as the excitement in the house grows. The dog will be barking, jumping, and biting the guest's or owner's clothes. Anything the owner does only makes the behavior worse. Whenever I am called in for a dog like this, I want to record the training session because I can literally see the dog let out a sigh of relief. It's almost as if he is saying, *"Thanks chief, I needed that."*

Please remember, punishment is NOT abuse. There is a big difference between abusing a dog and applying a negative consequence. Once the punishment has been applied, the dog will often look to the owner as the one with the highest status and everything in the house starts to calm down.

Tenet #5: Violence begets violence.

I agree, violence often does beget violence, but who the heck is talking about violence? Punishment is NOT violence. Again, the all positive crowd points to punishment and labels it violence. There is nothing violent about a dog on an underground containment system. There is nothing violent about a dog on an electronic or prong collar. There is nothing violent about a dog getting bonked with a towel. Instead of being intellectually honest, force-free trainers tell dog owners any form of negative consequence is a display of violence when nothing could be further from the truth.

Straight out of the Oxford Dictionary, violence is described as: *"behavior involving physical force intended to hurt, damage, or kill someone or something."* When a dog is being trained, there is no intention to hurt, damage, or kill the dog.

SCIENCE-BASED IS GOOD FOR BUSINESS

These are only five tenets of the Church of Positive Training, and there are many more. They are needed to round up members and demonize anyone who disagrees because marketing is a big part of running a dog training business. It's even more important when you are running a mass movement. You have to differentiate yourself from the competition and sell your idea to hordes of dog trainers. You must take a superior position and point to everyone else, labeling them the devil.

This is also good for a dog trainer's business. Dogs are an emotional issue. You have a dog owner who is very attached to his dog but the dog is exhibiting behaviors he doesn't like, sometimes dangerous behaviors. After all, don't forget dogs are predatory animals with strong jaws and sharp canines which can tear through flesh and bone.

So the owner takes a gander through the listings on Google. He has options and one of those is a trainer who is all positive, force-free, and science-based, who promises results without the harsh use of prong, choke, or electronic collars. The dog owner, who loves his dog, thinks, "*Wow, this must be the right choice,*" and is given a clear reason to pick up the phone and call this trainer. The dog owner wants the best for his dog and this is a good selling point. Why would he choose one of those other trainers when this all positive, force-free trainer claims he can help? Especially when there are some very abusive dog trainers out there. You can go to YouTube and find plenty of nasty trainers. You'll see dog trainers hanging dogs on choke collars, using electronic collars in an abusive way, and other awful, disgusting examples of training. I have been in this business for a long time and I was exposed to trainers that would make your skin crawl.

MY STINT WITH THE CHURCH

It was one of the reasons the Church of Positive Only Training was appealing to me in my younger days. I had seen first-hand how some dogs were treated in the name of training. I was also working as an Animal Control Officer for the city of Fall River in Massachusetts, a city of ninety thousand people and the amount of abuse and mistreatment would give you nightmares. I was also holding a lot of dogs down while they were being injected with a lethal dose of phenobarbital. It was heartbreaking and when I bumbled across the church it was something I felt I needed and whole-heartedly converted.

As a member, I followed the all positive mantra. The problem was I could never get the results the church promised. I did my best. I attended seminars and kept up to date on the latest and greatest protocols, but the more I learned and the more I applied only brought me closer to the understanding I would never be able to continue my career as a dog trainer. I couldn’t ignore the realization I wasn't really helping dog owners anymore. I had been a card-carrying member of the church and every day I knew I was not getting the results my clients were looking for. I also felt guilty because I was not completely faithful to the church. I was still recommending certain forms of punishment to stop behavior problems. I kept thinking I was not a very good trainer or a very good church member, and decided it was best to just leave the profession.

So, I sold my business (which offered boarding, grooming, daycare, and training) and bumbled around for about seven years trying different jobs to make a living. Nothing really caught on and one morning I woke up and realized I wanted to get back into dog training. This time though I was going to really learn what worked and was not going to follow any specific ideology. As I threw myself into the subject again, I was reminded training actually happens through using both positive and negative consequences. I also saw a negative consequence could be applied without adverse effects. I could have sold more books and I could have gotten more notoriety in the profession if I had stayed all positive and force-free, but my goal now is to help as many people as possible by clearing up all the confusion and exposing the myths surrounding dog training.

The biggest myth is using the term science-based when talking about all positive, force-free training. I hope after reading this chapter you will be skeptical about anyone who uses those words, or claims science proves anything. Science is very subjective.

CHAPTER 4

"An expert is the one who complicates simplicity."

Winston Churchill

Hey, No Letters Behind Your Name

How To Find A Dog Trainer And Why You Should Be Extremely Cautious If He Has Any Letters Next To His Name

I met with a potential client and she was trying to make the right decision before parting with her hard-earned money. I was not the only dog trainer she saw that day. How do I know? She told me. She then said something which made me laugh out loud. She said, *"You have no letters behind your name. I met with two other trainers and they both had letters behind their names."*

"I'm sorry I laughed," I said. *"I don't have any letters and probably never will and here's why..."*

You see, most people are unaware dog training is a completely unregulated profession. Over the past twenty or so years, some private organizations have developed tests and certifications, which upon passing, allow you to add some nifty little letters behind your name giving you an appearance of credibility. The reason I want nothing to do with the certifications offered is because these organizations have gone "positive reinforcement crazy." Now lean in real close because I need to make sure you hear me when I say this.

I love using positive reinforcement. I love being positive. I love positive people (like my wife!). I love doing fun and positive stuff with my dog. I try to be a positive father and friend. I read positive books and have been a fan of Zig Ziglar for more years than you can imagine and I even heard him speak live three times before he passed away.

BUT DOG TRAINING IS MORE THAN JUST USING POSITIVE REINFORCEMENT!!!

Dog training is using the right technique from the appropriate behavior quadrant at the correct time. If your dog is stealing food off the counter, you CAN'T use positive reinforcement unless you want your dog to steal more.

Here's a quick lesson:

There are four behavior quadrants we work from when using operant conditioning.

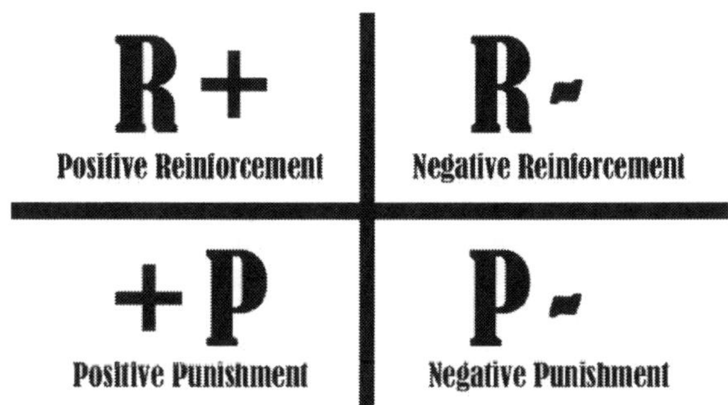

- Positive AND Negative Reinforcement are used to GET a behavior to occur.
- Positive AND Negative Punishment are used to STOP a behavior.

Reinforcement is used to increase the frequency of a behavior, and as much as you may wish you could use a clicker to STOP your dog from stealing food off the counter, it won't work. I know there are many who will argue with me, tell me you can teach the dog another behavior or redirect the dog, but I've yet to see it. I'm told all the time by church members it can be done, they can prevent a dog from stealing food using positive reinforcement but let me tell you, rewarding a dog in the presence of a chicken on the table does not mean the dog has learned to stop stealing people chow when the human has left the room.

While we would all love it if we could use positive reinforcement to stop a behavior, we have to understand dog training is not all sunshine and rainbows. We have to put on our big boy pants and provide training that actually works. We can't wish it wasn't the way it is. We have to use the right technique from the appropriate behavior quadrant at the correct time.

And this is different for each dog. My in-laws have a very sweet Cavalier King Charles Spaniel who likes to bark uncontrollably when people come over. The right technique could be a squirt of water because he's a sensitive little guy. So saying, QUIET, and squirting water the second he starts barking may be the right technique for him, from the correct quadrant (positive punishment), at the right time. However, a high-strung, easily overstimulated, nine-month-old chocolate lab will take a squirt of water to the face and probably enjoy it immensely. This would not be the right technique for the lab so you would have to find something different to effectively stop the behavior.

Let's go back to my statement about dog training becoming "positive reinforcement crazy" and what those letters really mean to you. One very popular TV trainer has created her own certification and with it you can get some nifty little letters and the power of a celebrity to back you up. If you are personally chosen by Victoria Stilwell to work with her, you can put the letters VSPDT behind your name. Isn't that special.

On her website she has four pillars of dog training. Here are the first two:

Pillar #1: The use of *positive reinforcement*

Holy cow! The use of positive reinforcement. Okay, I'm with you on that one Vicky. I use positive reinforcement when I want to teach a behavior. But what if I want to STOP a behavior? I have to use positive reinforcement? How is that accomplished?

Pillar #2: Avoiding the use of intimidation, physical punishment, or fear

This is where emotion kicks in and reason and logic make an exit out the back door. Before rejecting what I am about to say, please read it completely before passing any judgements.

Fear is a necessary and important emotion to live a normal, stable life. I am not talking about the chronic overwhelming fear and anxiety some people and dogs have to live with that requires professional help and medication. I am referring to the kind of fear that keeps you safe and healthy. Most people, when standing on a roof fifty feet up, feel a little fear as they walk out toward the edge. That fear keeps them from doing something stupid unless they're into drinking whisky and watching Jackass DVDs. Fear is what teaches you to look both ways when crossing a street. If you didn't fear getting smashed by a bus you probably wouldn't be here reading this. Fear, negative consequences, and punishment all provide information. This feedback is important to your well-being.

Fear and pain teach us valuable lessons all the time. It only takes once, maybe twice to figure out the pot inside the four hundred and fifty degree oven is hot and you should put oven mitts on to protect your hands and prevent a hospital visit for third degree burns. Getting burned is a negative consequence that happens every time you forget the potholders. The pain and fear you experience when your hands get charbroiled teaches you quickly how to avoid the negative consequence.

This is why her second pillar is dangerous. To refresh, Pillar #2 is: Avoiding the use of *intimidation, physical punishment, or fear.*

Every day we make decisions for our dogs. We have to decide the kind of medical care they are going to receive, the food they will eat, how often and what type of exercise they get to participate in, and most importantly, we have to keep them safe. Dogs that live on busy streets may get killed if allowed to freely roam and leave the yard whenever they desire. Even in a quiet neighborhood, a dog runs the risk of getting hit by a car.

Sure, some dogs have been completely freaked out by the use of electronic collars. There is NO arguing that. Teaching a dog with an electronic collar is more than just strapping it on and expecting it to work. There is an important conditioning phase the dog needs to go through first. But for some households, a physical fence is not an option, never mind many dogs have died from them. I've seen dogs try to jump fences only to get their collars caught and die from strangulation. So like anything in life, there are pros and cons.

Given the choice though, I would rather my dog receive a few unpleasant corrections from the collar than get hit by a car. I have discussed electronic containment systems a lot in this book for a reason. Watching your dog get hit and slide one hundred feet down a snowy street is impossible to forget. Running up and seeing his rib cage exposed from the road burn and his tongue hanging out dripping blood is a horrific scene for a ten-year-old boy to witness. All these years later the scene replays in my mind like it happened yesterday.

When I was ten, there were no underground electric fencing systems as far as I know. But if given the choice, I would have had ZERO hesitation to properly teach my dog to stay in the yard using punishment. My little beagle mix had no idea a van driving by at thirty miles an hour was going to end his life. Requiring trainers to *"avoid the use of intimidation, physical punishment, or fear,"* is unethical. It sounds nice, but to properly train your dog and keep him safe, you had best rethink following Vicky's advice.

As a kid, I was extremely lucky to grow up by the ocean. I literally spent every day on or in the water during the summer months. I learned to swim, snorkel, scuba dive, fish, sail, row, water ski, you name it. I loved all water sports and was extremely comfortable around water, too comfortable. One day when I was about seventeen, I had been water skiing with some friends. I wiped out a couple hundred yards from shore so I took off my life jacket, tossed it to my friends on the boat and told them I was going to swim in. They sped away and I started to swim towards shore, not realizing how fatigued I was. Soon I started to panic and thought I was going to drown. Luckily, I calmed down enough to slowly back stroke the rest of the way in, but my entire body was shaking when I hit dry land. That fearful experience was an important lesson I have never forgotten, and even to this day, I have a different level of respect when I am on or around water. The fear of drowning has made me much more cautious and safe around water.

So, before we finish off with the VSPDT accreditation, let's look at this little gem from her website:

"Science And Common Sense Say To Go Positive: Modern behavioral science has proven that dominance and punishment-based techniques employed by traditional 'old-school' dog trainers are less effective and more dangerous than science-based positive training. Our inner moral compasses, meanwhile, tell us that compulsions training just doesn't 'feel right' compared to positive reinforcement, especially when you begin to understand that positive methods actually work better anyway."

See, there they go, back to using science again...

It starts off with *"Modern behavioral science"* has proven punishment is less effective AND dangerous. So, if you use punishment you are putting the dog in danger? Really? As I have said over and over, punishment SAVES millions of dogs' lives every single day. A dog that no longer jumps will stay in the house. A dog that does not steal food off the counter will stay with the family. I have worked with shelters and as an Animal Control Officer and know dogs with behavior problems do not stay in their homes.

Now that we've talked about science, let's move onto our inner moral compass. Going from science to inner feelings. Yeah, I think this is how science works. I think this happened with Ivan Pavlov. I'm pretty sure he turned to his assistant and said, *"Hey Boris, now that we've discovered conditioned reflexes, what is your inner moral compass saying to you? Especially since we had to kill about thirty dogs to complete this experiment?"*

I know my inner moral compass says I have an ethical responsibility to do whatever possible to save a dog's life and solve the problem I am hired for.

This is why I have a big problem with dog trainers who have letters behind their names. If they stick to what they are taught and what Victoria wants them to do, THEY CAN ONLY WORK USING POSITIVE REINFORCEMENT. Is this really scientific? Or effective? Or ethical? She wants us to only work from one behavior quadrant and to let our inner moral compass decide what is the best course of action when it comes to training our dogs.

Are you starting to see why letters behind a name could actually backfire when you are looking to hire a dog trainer? And just so you don't think I am picking solely on Victoria, I have a bone to pick with most of the certifications for dog trainers.

The APDT has some pretty fancy alphabet soup you can put behind your name. This association belongs to the church and doesn't take kindly to any of its members talking about or using negative consequences. And to prove my point, here is what their code of ethics states:

To utilize training and behavior modification methods based on accurate scientific research, emphasizing positive relationships between people and dogs and using positive reinforcement-based techniques to the maximum extent possible.

The APDT is clearly against the use of punishment in training, and by pushing this agenda they are confusing dog trainers and the general public, which truly needs help bringing their dogs' behavior under control. The APDT has been pushing this ideology for so long, dog trainers now believe it hook, line, and sinker.

Here is what their code of ethics should say:

To utilize training and behavior modification methods based on accurate scientific research, emphasizing positive relationship between people and dogs and using the right technique from the appropriate behavior quadrant at the correct time including the use of "positive punishment" to stop or reduce a behavior.

The ADPT motto on their website is: "*Building better trainers through education,*" and then they go on to "educate" their members by pushing position statements like this:

"Dog-friendly training is training that utilizes primarily positive reinforcement; secondarily negative punishment, and only occasionally, rarely, and/or as a last resort includes positive punishment and/or negative reinforcement."

What a minute. Wait one cotton pickin' minute. According to the APDT, a trainer can use positive punishment when it is the last resort? When is this decided? Why wait? Are you going to spend hours, days, weeks, even months throwing cookies at the dog trying to counter-condition or redirect the behavior? Are you going to spend five years doing it?

Please let me state for the record one more time. I use positive reinforcement. I love using positive reinforcement. And I use it every time IT IS THE CORRECT TIME TO USE IT! I do NOT use positive reinforcement when I am dealing with barking, counter surfing, jumping, reactive behavior, or any other time I need the dog to STOP doing something. And by now the

Church of Positive Only Training is screaming this. I can hear it. This is the mantra from APDT: "*What do you want the animal TO do?*"

Here is their position statement: "*We focus on reinforcing desired behaviors, and always ask the question, 'What do you want the animal TO do?' when working through a training or behavior problem. Relying on punishment in training does not answer this question, and therefore offers no acceptable behavior for the animal to learn in place of the unwanted behavior. Punishment should never be the first line of treatment in an intervention, nor should it make up the majority of a behavior modification program. Further, it should be discontinued as quickly as possible once the desired behavior change has taken place.*

I'd like you to picture me at my desk with my face in my hands because this is what I am doing. By now you should understand why I am slowly shaking my head and using deep breathing exercises to calm down.

Imagine your friendly neighborhood dog trainer (me) walking into a house and once I enter there is a snarling, barking, lunging seventy-pound German shepherd being held back by her owner - barely. As a highly trained canine specialist hired to solve this particular behavior problem, let's start with what the APDT wants me to do. Ask myself the question, "*What do I want the dog TO do?*" What do I want the dog to do? Okay let's start with I'd like the German shepherd to stop lunging and barking at me. I'd also like to see less of the pointed teeth between the incisors and premolars, often referred to as canines. And if you think throwing treats at a snapping, growling adult German shepherd is going to work, you need to have your head examined. Besides, this dog has already refused treats. I need to get her to STOP barking fast. I need to get to the point where the owner can handle her - *FAST!*

I think I am going to go instead with the correct behavior quadrant - which is... positive punishment. And there goes my APDT Christmas Card. Off the list for good.

I know we're having some fun here, but this is a common situation I encounter and that was a real client and her dog. And in case you think I am making this up and just pushing my agenda, I filmed a video so you can watch me working with her. The beginning of the video was taken when I first walked into the house and documents Veeshka's initial response. I had to have her back tied because the owner was having difficulty holding her. In the first session, I stopped the barking and got her to be much more accepting of me walking into the house. This was accomplished in one session. You can see the video on my website, DeadlyDogTrainingMyth.com.

I understand why dog trainers so often confuse punishment with abuse. Over the years, some dog trainers have been pretty brutal and outright abusive with techniques they developed to produce desired behaviors like ear pinching, nail pulling, strangulation, etc. But this Church of Positive Only Training, that many top-name dog trainers and organizations belong to, is sending a lot of dogs on a one way trip to the vet's office, which is where Veeshka was headed.

This "positive reinforcement crazy" agenda is FLAWED. It's wrapped in a cloak of being nice and kind and scientific, but believe me when I say this, a dog who continues to jump and knock over people, a dog who barks non-stop, a dog who steals food, socks, and remotes, a dog who chases cars and bikes is in danger, big danger, and the way to save and help the dog is with a trainer who clearly understands and knows how to apply techniques from all four behavior quadrants.

So what do all those other letters mean? There are literally dozens of certifications dog trainers can get from all sorts of different organizations. Even individual well-known trainers hand out their own certifications to their devotees. So if you still are interested in those letters after a trainer's name, here are a few of the more popular:

ACDBC, Associate Certified Dog Behavior Consultant

This is awarded by the International Association of Animal Behavior Consultants which heavily promotes LIMA (Least Intrusive Minimally Aversive).

From their website: *"LIMA requires that trainers/behavior consultants work to increase the use of positive reinforcement and lessen the use of punishment in work with companion animals and the humans who care for them. LIMA protocols are designed to be maximally humane to learners of all species. In order to ensure best practices, consultants/trainers should pursue and maintain competence in animal behavior consulting through education, training, or supervised experience, and should not advise on problems outside the recognized boundaries of their competencies and experience."*

CBCC-KA, Certified Behavior Consultant Canine - Knowledge Assessed
CPDT-KA, Certified Professional Dog Trainer - Knowledge Assessed
CPDT-KSA, Certified Professional Dog Trainer - Knowledge & Skills Assessed

These certifications are all awarded by the Certification Council for Professional Dog Trainers (CCPDT).

From their homepage: *"The CCPDT is the leader in the development of rigorous exams to demonstrate mastery of humane, science-based dog training practices. They follow the Humane Hierarchy which states: "The standard of care for CCPDT certificants is that the Humane Hierarchy will be used as a guide in their decision making process when implementing training and behavior protocols. This standard of care should be followed when the certificant is working directly with a dog, creating a training plan for the client to follow, or assisting a colleague."*

DACVB, Diplomate of the American College of Veterinary Behaviorists

This certification is awarded by the American College of Veterinary Behaviorists (ACVB) and is recognized by the American Veterinary Medical Association (AVMA).

From the American Veterinary Medical Association website: *Punishment is not appropriate as a first-line or early-use treatment for behavior problems. Modification should focus on reinforcing desirable behaviors, removing reinforcement for inappropriate behaviors, and addressing the emotional state and environmental conditions driving undesirable behavior. The pitfalls and possible adverse effects of punishment include the following:*

- Timing punishment correctly is difficult.
- Punishment can strengthen the undesirable behavior.
- The punishment must be strong enough to be effective, but intense punishment can lead to physical harm.
- Regardless of the strength, punishment can cause some animals to become extremely fearful, and this fear can generalize to other contexts.
- Punishment can facilitate or even cause aggressive behavior.
- Punishment can suppress behaviors, including those behaviors that warn of aggression.
- Punishment can teach the animal to associate the owners, other animals, specific contexts, or environments with bad experiences.
- Punishment often does not address the underlying cause of behaviors or teach alternate behaviors.

Looks like our old friend, Anecdotal Evidence, has reared its ugly head again.

KPA CTP, Karen Pryor Academy Certified Training Partner

This certification is awarded by Karen Pryor Academy. According to their website, a trainer with this certification:

- Is skilled in using positive teaching and training techniques with you and your pet to make training fun.
- Is educated about using science and behavior-based methods to make training more efficient.
- Can customize a training program specifically designed to help you and your pet communicate and succeed together.
- Participates in programs for quality assurance and continuing education to ensure the training you receive is based on modern research and technology.
- Pledges to teach and train using force-free principles so you and your dog develop a bond built on trust and respect.

VSPDT, Victoria Stilwell Positively Dog Training

According to her website, this is a *"global network of hand-picked, world-class positive trainers. Victoria herself personally oversees the recruitment of the very best positive reinforcement dog trainers in the world to join her VSPDT team and bring the Positively mission of force-free positive training to the entire dog-loving world."*

THOSE LETTERS WONT' HELP YOU

So after reading this, you can see all the experts with fancy schmancy letters behind their names will have you spinning in circles for months because they won't use the correct course of action to STOP a behavior.

I helped a woman who was living in an apartment building with her little pit-mix that had developed a barking problem. This dog could not walk down the hallway without barking at anyone who passed. If someone knocked on the door, forget it, she would bark like crazy. The barking was so bad management sent a letter. The letter said the owner had better take care of the barking problem or the dog had to go. Here is where it gets interesting. The woman suffers from M.S. and said the dog was a therapy dog. The managers of the apartment building now had a tricky situation on their hands. They did not want to tangle with the American Association of People with Disabilities and they had to keep their other tenants happy.

Enter your friend and hero, the Amazing Dog Training Man. No fancy letters. Not a church member, just a dog trainer who knows how to help this dog and her owner, fortunately, a trainer who will use punishment to bring this behavior under control. The situation was about to get ugly. The lawyers were not far off. Let's stop for a minute and imagine if she hired a trainer with some fancy letters behind his name. He would have had to follow the guidelines put out by his accrediting organization.

So if that was the case, when does that trainer with the official looking letters get the all clear to use punishment to stop the behavior? The second session? The third? Fifth? After a lawsuit is filed? When? I'll tell you. Never. Church members do NOT use punishment because they do not know how to. It also goes against everything they believe in.

The Certification Council for Professional Dog Trainers uses the Humane Hierarchy which we talked about earlier.

A Diplomate of the American College of Veterinary Behaviorists has agreed: "*Punishment is not appropriate as a first-line or early-use treatment for behavior problems. Modification should focus on reinforcing desirable behaviors, removing reinforcement for inappropriate behaviors, and addressing the emotional state and environmental conditions driving undesirable behavior.*"

A trainer with a KPA CTP (Karen Pryor Academy Certified Training Partner) after her name "*pledges to teach and train using force-free principles so that you and your dog develop a bond built on trust and respect.*" Looks like no punishment allowed here. Their advice will be exercise, redirection, management, and when all else fails… blame the owner.

Victoria Stilwell's hand selected group of trainers agree to:

- ✓ Use Positive Reinforcement
- ✓ Avoid use of intimidation, physical punishment and fear
- ✓ Understand misconceptions about dominance theory
- ✓ Learn about the canine experience from the dog's POV

All these trainers will never fix the problem. So, you can see I could have an entire alphabet behind my name, I could be Eric Letendre, **ACDBC, CBCC-KA, DACVB, KPA CTP, CPDT-KSA, VSPDT** and even with all that, never know how to or be allowed to take care of the behavior problem. You may think I am kidding, but a trainer bestowed with any of these letters won't know how or be willing to fix your problem and instead will advise long, drawn out, utterly useless protocols.

So instead, my business card simply says: *Eric Letendre, Dog Trainer.* And my lowly status as just a dog trainer with no letters was able to help the women with the barking problem. The dog was fearful of people and was the reason for the barking. The dog would pass people, bark, and be removed from the situation. This would strengthen the behavior. Barking resulted in people moving away. The force-free trainers would tell you to NEVER, under any circumstances, use punishment on a fearful dog. Wrong! That is exactly what I did. The dog was doing a behavior that needed to be stopped. It does not matter what the underlying reason was and I can assure you, the dog would be much more fearful sitting in a cold kennel, waiting on an adoption that would likely never come, and eventually finding herself on a sterilized steel table with a vet ending her life.

So I used to punishment to stop the barking. The dog was able to quietly walk past strangers. We walked up to the apartment manager's office and showed her the results. This did not take weeks of counterconditioning and desensitization. It took one session.

CHAPTER 5

"Even if you are a minority of one, the truth is the truth."

Mahatma Gandhi

Confessions Of A Professional Dog Trainer

How The Only Positive Dog Training Mass Movement Has Confused Dog Owners And How To Find A Good Dog Trainer

In 1807, the most powerful man in the world was France's, Napoleon Bonaparte. After signing a treaty with Russia ending a war between the two countries, Napoleon thought a rabbit hunt would be a great way to celebrate. Little did he know, he and his men would be attacked and forced to retreat from the hunting fields. Here is what happened.

About three thousand rabbits were rounded up and dumped into the fields where Napoleon and his top brass were going to hunt. The rabbits were released from their cages and the hunt was on. But here is the strange part.

The rabbits didn't scurry away. Instead, thousands of fuzzy little bunnies headed straight at Napoleon and his posse. At first, Napoleon and his crew got a chuckle out of the charging bunnies, but the hordes of long-eared, furry little creatures didn't stop. They came straight on and went right up Napoleon's leg and he and his men were swarmed. After trying unsuccessfully to swat them away, they admitted they were swamped and knew there was only one course of action… retreat. Napoleon and his crew hopped in the coach and hauled butt out of there.

It's a strange but true story and here is why it happened. You see, the rabbits used for the hunt were gathered from local farmers and they were tame. They had no fear of humans. Instead, they saw them as waiters, bringing lunch every day. They had no manners, no respect, and their only thought when they saw Napoleon and his men was, *"FEED ME!"*

I have seen the same happen with dogs. Many look at their owners as their own personal chuck wagon and chew toy. This is why you must teach your dog manners. Your dog has to understand you are NOT just a food dispenser. I have met plenty of dogs that acted just like the rabbits going after Napoleon.

ALL DOGS NEED TO BE TRAINED

Behaviors that are natural and normal to dogs often times frustrate us. The main reason people hire me is to STOP unwanted behaviors. While I was teaching a class at a local veterinary practice, I asked everyone in the room if there were any questions. I knew what the questions were going to be. *"How do I stop my dog from jumping?" "How do I stop my dog from biting?" "How do I stop my dog from knocking over the kids?"* Most dog owners attend a class to learn how to stop their dog from doing something. SIT, DOWN, STAY, and COME are very important commands, but most of the time someone hires me to help get his dog under control. The only way to accomplish that is by using some form of negative consequence.

If your dog is driving you crazy, Google is probably the first place you went to for help. A quick search on any common behavior problem will result in many "positive" ways to correct it. For example, I searched for: "How to stop barking" and these were my top ten results:

1. How to Get Your Dog to Stop Barking : The Humane Society...
2. Cesar's best tips to stop dog barking | Cesar's Way
3. The Dog Trainer : How to Get Your Dog to Stop Barking Inside Quick ...
4. How To Quickly Stop Dog Barking - YouTube
5. Why Dogs Bark: Stop Excessive Barking - Pets - WebMD
6. Victoria Stilwell: How to Deal with Out-of-Control Barking | The Bark
7. How to Stop Unwanted Barking | Karen Pryor Clicker Training
8. How To Stop Dogs Barking - Tips & Advice | Love That Pet™
9. 5 Ways to Get Dogs to Stop Barking - wikiHow
10. Dog Barking, Puppy Barking - Perfect Paws

Here is what the top results from Google recommend. Let's take a look at their advice with my commentary in italics:

- Remove the motivation. *Remove all squirrels, cats, and leaves that may blow by and trigger your dog's barking Also make sure no one walks past your house. Insist your neighbor rehome their cat and adopt out their small children who like to play ball. This is completely impractical advice.*

- Ignore the barking. *Perfect! Fold your arms and ignore your dog's barking at 6:00 AM as your neighbor calls the police. You can ask him to stand there and ignore the barking with you. Heck, ask the entire neighborhood to please ignore your dog's barking. Completely useless advice.*

- Desensitize your dog to the stimulus. *This is the answer to every behavior problem from the Church of Positive Only Training. Desensitize your dog to anything that makes him bark. How the heck do you do that? Give your dog treats when he sees a squirrel or cat? Again, nothing here to help you.*

- Teach your dog the "quiet" command. *Okay, now we're on to something. But, HOW? How do we teach quiet? (I'll show you soon.)*

- Ask your dog for an incompatible behavior. Incompatible behavior is identifying a **behavior** that's **incompatible** with, or cannot occur at the same time as the problem **behavior**. The focus is on replacing negative **behaviors** with positive **behaviors**. *Okay, what behavior can't occur at the same time as the barking? What behavior can replace barking? Sit? Stay? Down? Give paw? Um, I'm pretty sure my dog can still bark in any of these positions.*

- Keep your dog tired. *How tired? How much exercise can I give him every day? I have three kids in karate, dance, and tuba lessons. I already walk my dog twice a day and put him in daycare three times a week.*

This list put out by the Humane Society is nearly identical to all the other advice given in the top ten results except for Love That Pet and Cesar Milan.

The Love That Pet website recommends keeping a Barking Diary. The Barking Diary is to see if there is any noticeable pattern to your dog's barking. Most of the dog owners I work with would look at me like I had three heads if I recommended this. They would also probably say: "*Who cares what my dog's barking pattern is? I want the dog to shut the #@%! up.*" Love That Pet website also recommend a Husher which is a muzzle to put on your dog to control the barking. For safety reasons, I never recommend any type of muzzle on an unsupervised dog.

Cesar recommends: "*Correct dog problem behavior and follow through. Tell your dog to stop barking using a look, a sound, or a physical correction. But don't stop there. Your dog may pause and then go right back to what he was doing. His body relaxed, but his brain was still on alert. Be patient. Wait until your dog submits before you go back to what you were doing.*" Cesar is not specific about what kind of physical correction, but he is the only one who recommends it.

I use barking as an example because it can be a big problem. Even if Animal Control or the police don't get involved, you will get uninvited from the neighborhood block party if your dog is barking at three in the morning. No one loves hearing unending, loud barking. We all love dogs, but barking is a behavior that will set your teeth on edge, and it is your responsibility to make sure your dog is not being a nuisance.

Finding a good trainer (or the right advice online) can be confusing. On one hand, some trainers feel you should never use food and dogs should comply just because you said so. On the other side of the spectrum, you have trainers who will want you to always throw treats at your dog. How do you know who to listen to? This is a big problem for dog owners. I'm going to try to clear some of the confusion up for you.

WHAT ABOUT GROUP CLASSES?

If you have a puppy, a group puppy class can be a good idea. It will allow your dog to socialize with other friendly puppies and get a good start on learning behaviors, however, if you sign up for a group obedience class with a barking dog, you will most likely be asked to leave. And if you have a behavior problem you'd like solved, I probably wouldn't even recommend a group class. They can be good for teaching behaviors but most likely, the instructor can't or won't help you with common behavior problems like barking.

After an initial online search, the next step most dog owners take is attending a group obedience class. They sign up with hopes of finding the answers to make their dogs behave. They want to learn how to teach their dogs to do obedience commands but mostly, they want to get Sparky under control. The problem with a group class is you will only learn how to teach your dog to DO behaviors. Your typical class will either be taught by a church member or an "old school" instructor who will issue you a choke or prong collar on day one. Either way, group classes can create a lot of problems, and if you attend an all positive class, your behavior problems will not be corrected.

In other words, if you need your dog to STOP doing behaviors, you are out of luck. An all positive trainer can't help you because behaviors can't be stopped with treats. All the counterconditioning, desensitization, and extinction in the world will not solve your jumping, barking, chewing, biting, or counter surfing problems. On the other hand, if you go to an old school trainer using choke or prong collars, your dog could walk out with some new major problems. Let me explain why.

Corrections were often the only way old school trainers taught obedience. Every dog would be issued a choke or prong collar and treats were never used. There are good old school trainers but many of them were very harsh. They fueled the mass movement for the Church of Positive Only Training. The problem with using a prong or choke collar in a class setting is it can create superstitious behaviors, also known as cross associations.

I started under an old school trainer. At the beginning of each new class, I would watch a group of twenty happy, out of control, exuberant dogs walk in. Everyone would be issued a choke chain. The collar would be put on and the corrections would begin. There was no positive reinforcement and no fun. It was all business. And if a dog pulled towards another class member, he'd receive a heavy correction. This is where a choke or prong collar can become such a problem in a group setting.

Say your dog sees another dog and pulls to say Hi and sniff butts. You give a correction because your dog is pulling. He then associates the correction with the dog he is looking at. If this happens a few times, your dog will generalize the behavior. He'll start to think, *"The sight of other dogs equals a correction. Sight of other dogs... not good."* Your dog then becomes aggressive around strange dogs. Not exactly what you were looking for when you signed up for class.

In a group setting, you need to control your dog. I often use Gentle Leaders because they can quickly get the most difficult, out-of-control, hard-pulling dog under control. They are not for every dog, but using one will help control your dog. A Gentle Leader does not teach your dog to walk with you, but it will manage his behavior. A prong collar will help you teach your dog to walk with you, but you need to spend some time conditioning him to the collar.

Don't make the mistake of confusing the Gentle Leader with the Easy Walk Harness, which has become all the rage with the Church of Positive Only Training. The church members rave about the Easy Walk Harness, and like most things the force-free crowd pushes, the Easy Walk Harness doesn't work too well. If you want your dog to pull, by all means, strap on the harness, but if you want control, go with the Gentle Leader. If you want to walk your dog with ease, if you want command in every situation, trust me, use a Gentle Leader or a prong collar. And if you have a reactive dog, a dog who likes to lunge and pull at the sight of other dogs, you definitely need to start using a Gentle Leader. With the Gentle Leader, you will never need to worry about cross associations and will have instant control.

Reward based training is not without its own problems in a group setting. I just came from a client's house where one of her two dogs, a twenty pound little mixed-breed, blows a gasket every time she sees another dog. She attended a few group obedience classes looking for help with this problem because she and her husband love to go walking with both dogs. They live in Bristol, Rhode Island near Colt State Park, which is a beautiful place to walk any time of the year. In class, she was told by the instructor to use treats to distract her dog when she started barking at the other dogs. In this case, her dog was constantly getting rewarded for barking at other dogs. They positively reinforced barking, creating an out of control, off the hook behavior when another dog was around.

Her little dog was one of the loudest barking dogs I've ever heard. In all my years, I don't think I've ever seen quite the frenzy this little girl created around other dogs. I completely understood why the owner no longer walked her dogs. It was too embarrassing. Her dog would go ape s#@%! and the only way to stop it was by picking her up and walking away. The positive reinforcement approach created the same undesirable effect as the choke and prong collars. The behavior was reinforced and rewarded and it got to the point where it became out of control. By the time I met with her, she had been dealing with this problem for two years.

HOW DO YOU FIND A TRAINER?

So, what to do, where to go? Well, veterinarians can be a place to start when looking for a good dog trainer. There should be someone in your area who has a good reputation and has helped solve their clients' behavior problems. Once you find a dog trainer, ask if you can observe a class or ask for references from happy clients. This is not foolproof but it is start. Social media makes it easy for dog trainers to put up some videos of the dogs they have worked with. The videos should show before and after results, much like the ones I share on my YouTube channel, Facebook page, and on my website, DeadlyDogTrainingMyth.com. The videos should also give you a sense of the trainer's personality to help you determine if you'd like to work with that person.

In my business, I always meet with the dog owner first before any money is exchanged for a free behavior evaluation. This way, the dog owner can spend some time with me, I get a better idea of what I'll be dealing with, and we have a chance to make sure we can work together because this is a two way street. It doesn't happen too often, but on occasion, I do come across someone who I have no desire to take on as a client.

Patience is another very important quality in a trainer. A good sense of humor helps too, but is not necessary. Most important though, you should always be treated with respect. Believe it or not, there are a lot of dog trainers who are not very nice to their clients. I think this happens because aspiring dog trainers are under the false assumption they will get to play with dogs all day and not have to deal with people.

The reality is quite the opposite. A pet dog trainer's job IS working with people because all dogs getting trained have owners on the other end of the leash. I love my clients, human and canine, and enjoy working with them. I believe I have the best job on the planet. Every day I get to meet new people and their dogs. The greatest part of my job is seeing how happy my clients are when I help solve a difficult problem. If any dog trainer talks down or demeans you, do not part with your hard-earned money. There are many wonderful dog trainers out there to help you, but if you come across any who think they walk on water because they train dogs, tell them to take a hike. Also, if you do not feel comfortable with what the dog trainer is doing, speak up. A good trainer will explain everything he is going to do and then ask if you are okay with it. If you have a trainer who thinks he can do whatever he wants with your dog, tell him to move on.

THE MOST IMPORTANT QUESTION TO ASK

Like I've said before, stopping a behavior is the main reason most people contact a dog trainer. A good trainer will be able to get you quick results for common behavior problems. Jumping, stealing, biting, and other behaviors can be stopped within a session or two. An important question to ask before hiring any dog trainer is, *"How do you stop a behavior?"* A good trainer will show you the exact way to stop the annoying behaviors you have been living with.

Remember, there is a huge mass movement of all positive dog trainers roaming the planet and they believe with religious fervor, punishment should NEVER be used. They devoutly believe you can only use positive, reward-based methods which will DO NOTHING to help you with common behavior problems like jumping, barking, and so on. All the fancy terms they might throw out when answering your question, like counterconditioning and desensitization, are used to dazzle and confuse you. If you like that sort of stuff and are not looking for results, work with this type of trainer. If you truly want the bad behavior to end, I would suggest you keep looking.

Asking questions is the way to get the most out of any class you take. I have been teaching classes for a long time. By now, I have taught hundreds of classes and have worked with thousands of dogs. I encourage questions and provide practical answers. Most of the people listen to me and apply what I teach. Occasionally, some people have their own ideas and think their dogs can reason like a human. That would be fun, but unfortunately, they can't, so, if you encourage your dog to jump, your dog will jump. He won't care if you are wearing sweatpants and a T-shirt or a three-piece suit. If you encourage your dog to play bite by roughhousing, he'll think it's ok to play that way with anyone he comes in contact with.

I remember a few years back I was teaching an obedience class and a couple was in attendance with their six-month-old German shepherd. Over the course of the next hour, I watched this guy continuously push at his dog's head, encouraging his pup to bite his hands. He must have been doing it unconsciously because at the end of class the couple approached and asked for a few minutes of my time. The guy then said they have a biting problem. Their pup bites everyone in the house, the kids, his wife, him. He even added it had become a real serious problem and they would like it to stop. I stood there speechless for a few seconds and my first word was… *"Really?"* He gave me a strange look so I told him I had just watched him encourage his dog to bite for the past sixty minutes. He chuckled and said his playing had nothing to do with the biting problem.

So here is the main point to keep in mind when you're looking for dog training advice online, a trainer to work with, or a class to attend: Dogs only do two types of behavior. They do behaviors we like and behaviors we don't like.

To get more of the behaviors we like such as SIT, DOWN, STAY, and COME, it's most effective to use positive reinforcement. When you want to teach a behavior, use rewards. Use treats, praise, toys, and anything your dog likes to reinforce a behavior. Clickers and markers can be especially helpful with training.

Now to get less of the behaviors you don't like such as jumping, biting, barking, growling, digging, etc., you need to use a negative consequence, also known as punishment. And please remember: punishment is NOT abuse. Punishment is information necessary to teach your dog how to live with humans. Thinking you can solve behavior problems with positive reinforcement is only going to frustrate you both.

DOG TRAINING IS NOT ROCKET SCIENCE

Practical, useful dog training advice is what dog owners need today. Understanding behavior is not rocket science unless you listen to the self-proclaimed experts. Most of them are ideologues who follow a belief system that does not help dogs or their owners. They can't fix behavior problems using positive reinforcement so they develop complicated protocols that take months to work through, that still don't work (but by that time they can blame the owner for not following the protocol correctly).

One of the biggest problems I see today is reactivity on leash. There are so many dogs who lose their marbles when they see another dog or person.

This is a very difficult type of dog to own. He always keeps you on guard and doesn't allow you walk him. There are many training protocols developed around this problem. BAT, CAT, LAT, and Click to Calm are just a few and are very popular among the all positive crowd. Following these methods takes months. They all have the dog work "under threshold," never allowing him to get close to other dogs. They use fake dogs as decoys, curtains the dog has to stand behind, and keep other dogs up to one hundred yards away (if you want a visual, that's the length of a football field), gradually, slowly, working the dogs closer and closer.

Can you imagine how long it would take to get from one end of a football field to the other, always working under threshold? What dog owner has that amount of time or patience to train his dog to simply take a walk down the street without blowing a gasket? Most of the reactive dog problems I work with are corrected the first day. You can see the results on DeadlyDogTrainingMyth.com. All the dogs were brought under control using a simple training technique which gets the dog to focus on the owner instead of the other dog.

CHAPTER 6

"In nature there are neither rewards nor punishments; there are consequences."

Robert Green Ingersoll

The Positive Power OF A Negative Consequence

Teaching Your Dog NO Is More Powerful Than Teaching Your Dog YES

Sarah McLachlan's song, "Angel," starts playing in the background as you're watching TV and you hear the words, *"Every hour... an animal is beaten or abused..."* The camera then cuts to a frightened dog staring at you with sad eyes. Next a scared cat with a slight shake peers out of your TV. The words, *"They suffer alone and terrified,"* flash across the screen with the camera continuing to pan across the faces of dogs behind bars, *"Waiting for someone to help."* An older dog gingerly gets off the bed and limps across the floor. By this time you're getting choked up and realize what you're watching is actually painful. What you've witnessed is an ASPCA advertisement. Writer Kelly Conaboy writes in a December 28, 2015 NYMag.com article, "*Sarah McLachlan's "Angel"-scored ASPCA commercials are without a doubt the most difficult ads to watch on television.*"

Yet, every church member on the planet will endorse this commercial, even though it is using pain and fear to motivate. This commercial perfectly illustrates the positive power of a negative consequence. Consider this: Why do these advertisements always use the same format? They are very sad, even painful for the viewer. Why don't they show dogs living in happy new forever homes? Why don't they show the adopted dogs romping around the backyard with the kids, playing ball? I'll tell you. Because using an all positive commercial will not round up the donations like a negative one will. I am in no way knocking this approach to fundraising. They have to make them work. It costs big bucks to hire an ad agency, produce it, and then run it on national television. An all positive ad wouldn't bring in enough donations to keep the lights on.

The point I'm illustrating is the positive power of negative consequences. The negative commercials the ASPCA airs help roundup big bucks for the organization. And by big bucks I am talking close to thirty million dollars. In a December 2008 NY Times article, Stephanie Strom described it as, "*a landmark in nonprofit fundraising, where such amounts are virtually unimaginable for a single commercial.*" I hope by now you are starting to see why some of the most important lessons your dog will learn come from negative consequences.

The commercial is actually using negative reinforcement. Remember, when it comes to behavior you have four quadrants. There is positive reinforcement, positive punishment, negative punishment and negative reinforcement. Positive punishment and negative punishment are used to STOP behaviors. Positive reinforcement and negative reinforcement are used to GET behaviors to occur.

You can get a dog (or person) to DO a behavior using either positive or negative reinforcement. If I was waiting at a light behind a car and the light was green, I could walk up to the driver and offer a free cup of coffee if they moved or I could blast my horn until they moved. Negative reinforcement gets a bad rap but it is important to keep things in perspective. Negative reinforcement keeps you safe and helps avoid harm. When you put an oven mitt on to remove the casserole from the oven, negative reinforcement is at work. You are DOING a behavior. You put the glove on to avoid the painful experience of grabbing the three hundred and fifty degree pan. This is another example of the positive power of negative consequences at work.

The ASPCA has about sixty seconds to get you to put down the can of beer, move away from the nachos, pick up the phone, call, take your credit card out, and make a donation. This is no small task. Positive reinforcement won't cut it but negative reinforcement does the trick every time. All the pictures in the world of happy dogs and new families walking out of the shelter, statistics about how many dogs are saved, and positive quotes don't cut it. Negative reinforcement, in this situation, is much more compelling. Otherwise we would see only happy commercials.

This will be the most controversial chapter in the book because it goes against conventional dog training wisdom. Even in our own lives, most of the information we are bombarded with regularly encourages us to stay positive, think positive, BE POSITIVE! Positive thinking is the mantra everyone hears on a daily basis. And I am all for being, thinking, and feeling positive. I've been a fan of Zig Ziglar and Norman Vincent Peale tapes and books since my teens, but I have learned there are huge misconceptions surrounding the whole "Think and Be Positive Movement." When something bad or negative happens to me, as much as I don't like it, as much as it may be painful, it provides information which CAN ACTUALLY HELP ME!

Our environment is constantly providing us with information. If we choose to ignore that information, it could create problems in our life. When you see storm clouds, smoke, or any other warning signal, you can take this information and use it to keep yourself safe. The consequences we use to teach our dogs to do behaviors or to stop behaviors are valuable to him. He can store this information and remember it for future reference to learn how to live harmoniously with humans.

Teaching NO is more important than teaching YES. Insane is how this statement will be described by many. You may even be thinking I am crazy and just trying to be controversial but I stand by it. Let me repeat, teaching NO is more important than teaching YES. Let me explain by first asking a few questions. What is more important to you? A dog who knows DOWN or a dog who hits the brakes at the front door and won't go past the threshold? I'd say a dog who stops at the door is much safer. Would you rather a dog who knows the SIT command or a dog who does not touch the garbage? A dog that knocks over the garbage and drags trash all over the floor and eats old chicken bones is going to get into hot water. Even worse, eating chicken bones could cost thousands in surgery or possibly death. SIT is a nice command to know, but it is often more important to teach your dog to stop doing behaviors.

Robert Ringer is one of my favorite authors. He wrote some great books that I highly recommend. Mr. Ringer has a personal philosophy I admire and try to follow in my own life. He writes, "*Reality isn't the way you wish things to be, nor the way they appear to be, but the way they actually are. People say they love truth, but in reality they want to believe that which they love is true. If you are prepared, then you are able to feel confident.*"

This is such a great quote because so many people say they want the truth but in my experience, that's often not the case. In the dog training world, the church members want dog training to be one way and they definitely don't want to admit what is true. They can't face the fact that all dogs should learn the word NO. In reality, there is no getting around it. If you want your dog to be safe, if you want your dog to stop doing behaviors, you must use some form of negative consequence. Instead of facing up to this fact, they come up with all sorts of explanations on why punishment is abusive, how the dog will develop fear problems, aggression problems, and so on.

And please remember: Punishment is NOT abuse. Absence of punishment is not good for a dog. He will get incomplete information, which will result in more unwanted behavior, potentially ending at a shelter or worse. So the fact remains: Teaching your dog NO is more important than teaching YES, and that's reality.

Sometimes people accuse me of being pro punishment when nothing could be further from the truth. I am only interested in helping dogs and their owners get the results they need to have a harmonious relationship. Punishment does NOT need to be painful, or hurt the dog in any way. It simply provides information.

Being a huge Seinfeld fan, I'm reminded of this great scene where Jerry is at a restaurant getting ready to have dinner. Before the meal is served, he goes into the bathroom and while standing at the urinals, the chef comes in and pees next to Jerry. When he is finished, he touches up his hair and walks out. Jerry is flabbergasted. He can't believe the chef didn't wash his hands. Back at his table, when dinner is served he refuses to eat his meal. His girlfriend is annoyed and can't figure out why Jerry won't touch his food. This is an example of punishment that did not hurt, cause pain, or be abusive. Jerry used the information from his environment to stop doing a behavior he thought would be harmful to him. Eating food prepared by someone who did not wash his hands could make Jerry sick. This is a classic form of punishment. The chef not washing his hands STOPPED Jerry from eating.

Punishment STOPS behavior! In this situation, food is the aversive. Food is repulsive to Jerry. Even if Jerry's girlfriend ordered his favorite dessert, it wouldn't matter because at this time, ALL FOOD is disgusting to him. So much for using treats to solve every problem.

My first house was attached to my business. Half of the building was for business use and the other half was my residence. The day of the closing the fire inspector came to the house and said he would not sign off because he wanted me to get another fire alarm! I was beside myself with anger. Another fire alarm? I already had two in the house and he wanted another. I had a million things to do the day of the closing and now I had to run down to Home Depot and get another stinking fire alarm.

Fast forward a year and my fish tank (yes, fish tank) caught on fire. I was not at home but my girlfriend at the time was. She was in the business section of house, and heard the very alarm I complained about. She ran to the residence and contained the fire as best she could until the fire department arrived. By the time I got there, I could not believe the amount of smoke damage it caused. If she had not heard the alarm, the damage would have been even greater. The punishment inflicted on me by the fire inspector (not signing off on the closing) was the best thing that could have happened to me that day. If he had instead offered me a reward for installing a third fire alarm, I would have put it off and a fire would have destroyed my house and business. I hope by now you can see why I say punishment does not need to be painful, it is just information used to keep you and your dog safe.

E-Collars or shock collars are often pointed to as the most abusive type of training tool around. Make no mistake, shock collars can be used for evil purposes. It won't take long to do a search on YouTube to find a trainer abusing some poor dog with a shock collar. But then again, a knife can be used to cut your food or stab someone to death. Like a knife, an E-Collar is just a tool. Don't be fooled into thinking they are evil. Every day they save dogs' lives. A positive outcome is achieved through a negative consequence.

The underground containment systems used by millions of dog owners all over the country are safely containing dogs in their yards through the use of electronic collars. There is no denying Invisible Fence allows for a better quality of life and the amount of stress and worry on the owner is reduced once the dog learns to stay safely within the boundaries. The force-free crowd will claim there are side effects and call it is the worst way to keep your dog in the yard but take a quick ride around your neighborhood. I can guarantee you'll see plenty of happy, well-behaved dogs on the other side of the invisible barriers. Your dog can learn to stay in the yard in a quick, safe, and efficient manner with an electronic collar.

FORCE-FREE IS NOT THE ANSWER

Force-free dog training has become a very popular way of promoting your business and many dog trainers now tell unsuspecting dog owners force-free is the only way to train. It became popular around 2012 when the Pet Professional Guild was formed. This is from their homepage:

The Pet Professional Guild is a membership organization representing pet industry professionals who are committed to results based, science based force-free training and pet care. Pet Professional Guild Members Understand Force-Free to mean: No Shock, No Pain, No Choke, No Fear, No Physical Force, No Compulsion Based Methods are employed to train or care for a pet.

I agree it sounds wonderful, but it is false and misleading. First, there is no such thing as force-free dog training. If you put a leash or collar on your dog you are no longer force-free. Try training a dog without a leash or collar. Sure, it might work with some dogs, like one in ten thousand, but I would bet your dog will not stick with you without a leash or collar. So using a leash, collar, crate, baby gates, or tether is not force-free. Next… since only positive reinforcement can be used, you'll never stop behaviors. This is an organization which lives in a world where reality has flown out the window.

Not only is it misleading, but when you do try to train your dog with ***ONLY*** positive reinforcement and treats, the dog turns into a giant, spoiled brat. Think I'm kidding? I have been called in to work with so many dogs that have had treats thrown at them for everything. The biggest problem is with dogs that are reactive and freak out around other dogs. Counterconditioning and treats only make the very behavior they are trying to solve worse because the behavior is being rewarded. It's like another Seinfeld episode. It makes as much sense as wearing the pants you are returning:

KRAMER: No, I slipped - and fell in the mud. Ruining the very pants I was about to return.

ELAINE: (Reflects on the story) I don't understand.. you were wearing the pants you were returning?

KRAMER: Well, I guess I was.

ELAINE: (Still confused) What were you gonna wear on the way back?

KRAMER: Elaine, are you listening?! I didn't even get there!

No, I give my dog a treat every time he barks or growls at another dog.

I don't understand… you reward your dog for the behavior you want to stop?

Well, I guess I do.

Positive and negative consequences need to be thought of in a different way because positive is not always good and negative is not always bad. They are simply consequences, providing critical information to help your dog learn what is acceptable and what is unacceptable. Every week I work with dogs where the owners have spent good money on training, only to see their dogs' behaviors get worse.

I worked with a doodle that had developed a serious possession and food bowl problem. The owners had taken the puppy to class and during one of the sessions some toys were handed out. When the owners went to take the toy away, the puppy bit the owner on the hand. The trainer, a full-fledged church member, advised the owners to counter condition the puppy and use treats to calm her down. The behavior continued to worsen until I was called in at around a year. This dog now had a very serious problem. You must understand aggression is a normal, natural behavior for dogs. A dog, as it approaches physical maturity, will start to use aggression as a strategy. Since dogs are predatory animals with large teeth and strong jaws, your job is to make sure he learns it is unacceptable to bite or use his teeth in any way. The puppy should have been punished when she first started exhibiting the behavior.

We want to achieve harmony with our dogs. We want to live a happy, stress-free existence with our pups. When I first meet with a new client, I always make a list of behaviors they want to stop. For some clients, the list is short, for others it is long. I then ask what life would be like with their dogs once the problems they listed went away. The answers always amuse me. No one says, "*That would be good.*" The answers are always more like, "*I would love this dog sooooo much more. It would be awesome. If I could just solve these problems my life would be soooooo much easier.*"

In the last chapter, I talked about the little mixed breed that had the loudest, most obnoxious bark I've ever heard. It was so bad the owner had not walked her dog in public for two years. When she had attended a group obedience class taught by an all positive instructor, they were both put behind a barrier so the dog couldn't see the other dogs. They spent the entire class behind the barrier. Why? Because the instructor didn't know what to do to fix the problem.

The correct course of action would have been to apply a negative consequence to STOP the behavior. Once the behavior was stopped, the dog could have been brought into the class and taught with positive reinforcement. When I was hired, I showed her within fifteen minutes how to get her under control around other dogs. She told me she would have paid me any amount to get the barking under control. After three, quick negative consequences, her dog was calm and quiet around other dogs. Everyone's life is better.

Long, exhausting counter conditioning and desensitization is what the all positive, force-free trainers recommend. When that doesn't work, they'll have you resort back to management. They did not know how to stop the barking behavior so they tried to manage it. They put the dog behind a barrier in class to help manage the behavior, and this is what a lot of dog owners end up doing for long periods. Their dogs spend a lot of time in crates or inside houses, not getting the physical and mental stimulation all dogs need.

Dogs who are trained by the church members live a boring, uneventful life. When the owner spends months trying to use methods WHICH WILL NOT WORK, they give up and confine the dog. What else can they do? Some of the dogs are even brought to a shelter or put to sleep. It still amazes me that anyone would choose death over discomfort. I put the dog in a little discomfort (not pain) for a split second to stop the behavior. I had to repeat the negative consequence three times and now that dog's quality of life has been expanded exponentially. It's not just a little better, it's a huge improvement.

"But... but... but when punishment is used the dog's cortisol levels skyrocket and the dog's adrenaline shoots up making it very stressful on the dog," I can hear the church members lamenting. Funny, but it's actually the other way around. Think about a reactive dog on leash. Every time that dog walks out the door his cortisol and adrenaline will shoot up and stay there with every reactive encounter.

When I am working with a reactive dog, or a dog that jumps, bites, or displays any other excitable behavior, the dog actually calms down after I apply a negative consequence. You can see the visible change as the dog relaxes. It's as if you've given him permission to calm down and settle. Any adrenaline or cortisol drops and the great thing is when the dog calms down, you can get information into his brain. When a dog is out of control, there is no way you can train him. And if you think throwing a treat at a dog who is jumping and acting crazy at the front door is a good idea, you are just rewarding the very behavior you are trying to eliminate. It's much better to give a quick, painless, negative consequence and be done with it.

Both punishment and reinforcement need to be used with dogs. As I said over and over, they provide information for your dog so he knows what he can AND can't do. Just as important as using and teaching NO with a negative consequence, you must use and teach YES with a positive consequence.

The little barking dog was given three negative consequences to stop freaking out at the sight of other dogs. Once the behavior was stopped, we then used a clicker to reward her for walking past or being calm in the presence of other dogs. After two training sessions, they were able to take both of their dogs for a walk at a nearby state park with no barking, pulling, or uncontrollable behavior.

If you were to look at the ratio of treats given during our two sessions to negative consequences, there would be no comparison. She received dozens and dozens of treats to reward her for being well-behaved around other dogs. To try and ONLY use treats and positive reinforcement would have accomplished nothing. She would still be kept away from other dogs and the problem wouldn't have been solved. The dog and owner would still be sitting in the house.

Behavior is always compelled by consequences. If you have options, you won't always do what is in your best interest. Negative reinforcement has been used on humans for years to save lives. There is a difference between punishment and negative reinforcement. Since we are discussing the use of negative consequences for positive outcomes I want to show you how negative reinforcement (something else the all positive crowd freaks out about) is used every day, millions of times around this country to save lives.

Punishment is a consequence used to STOP a behavior. Negative reinforcement is something that is applied to get a behavior to occur. Every time you get in your car a bell or buzzer goes off until you put your seatbelt on. The simple, annoying bell helps compel you to do a behavior. This is an example of negative reinforcement and it saves lives. Given the choice, most people wouldn't use their seatbelts. After the last few years of using negative reinforcement along with stricter seat belt laws, wearing seatbelts has increased and saves millions of lives every year.

Are you starting to see why we need to stop promoting force-free and all positive and how ridiculous it is to keep pushing this agenda? It's time we start to look at behavior for what it is. Negative reinforcement does NOT need to be bad, it does NOT need to be painful.

Fear is good for you. I know this sounds shocking but fear keeps you safe and I can prove it. I am not talking about the fear which keeps you up all night or causes GI issues. What I am talking about is the fear you get from experience. I worked as a roofer back in the eighties. Roofing back then was brutal, hot, and dangerous. You would haul heavy shingles up a ladder and then try to balance as you heaved shingles around and nailed them into the plywood. When I worked as a roofer, there were no safety lines and the safety training was simple. My boss said, if you start sliding down the roof turn your hammer around and with the claw end, slam it into the roof. Hold yourself there and we'll get you help. That was it. Chances were, if you worked on a roof long enough, a fall was inevitable. If you were lucky, it was a short fall. Fear of falling while on the roof kept you from doing stupid things. Fear is why you look both ways before crossing a street. This is good! This is the positive power of a negative consequence. Negative consequences KEEP YOU SAFE.

To have a slogan which states: No Pain, No Force, No Fear could mean No Life. It's a dangerous slogan to promote. I believe I have a moral obligation to provide my clients with the correct information to help them. Most dog trainers today are following a flawed ideology fueled on emotion and fake science.

FEARFUL DOGS

Working with fearful dogs can be heartbreaking. The dog literally lives all day long in imagined terror. There is no actual threat but the dog believes he could die. It is an awful way to live. To help the fearful dog we must look at the behavior quadrants. Positive punishment and negative punishment are NOT used. These two quadrants are for STOPPING behaviors. The other two quadrants are positive and negative reinforcement. Naturally we would think positive reinforcement would help the fearful dog. Let's offer the dog treats, toys, verbal or physical praise, anything to help overcome the fear.

The problem? The terrified dog could care less about any of the above. Fear cancels out food, toys, praise, or anything else you can think of. So if positive reinforcement can't do the job, what are we left with?

I can hear it now, church members crying out, "*There is NO way you would use negative reinforcement on a fearful dog!!!*"

In reality, in order to get results, negative reinforcement IS the way to go and the best tool in many cases is...

Hold on a sec, I'll get back to the best tool in a moment. But first, ask yourself, "*Would you use negative reinforcement and break the cycle of terror or would you continue to let the dog live in constant fear?*" Remember, negative reinforcement does NOT have to be painful. Seeing fearful dogs put to sleep because no one could help them is NOT an option for me. When positive reinforcement does not work, I use negative reinforcement to help the dog.

By now you should understand that negative reinforcement saves lives. The bell that annoys you in your car to put on your seatbelt has saved millions of lives and made buckling up a habit. A chest pain compels you to see your doctor. Negative reinforcement results in a positive outcome. The seatbelt saves the person in the accident, the chest pain helps the person avoid a heart attack, the oven mitt prevents a third degree burn, the electronic collar helps the dog overcome his fear.

Yes, the electronic collar can and does help the fearful dog. Electronic collars today have many settings. The setting can be programed to a point where there is no pain, only sensation. The dog does feel the sensation from the collar and this can actually be used to help a fearful dog.

When positive reinforcement can't do the job, negative reinforcement will, much like the ASPCA commercial. Negative reinforcement is used to get the donations to pour in. You have to suspend your personal feelings for a moment and hear me out. A leash and electronic collar, used correctly, together help the dog get through the fear.

I worked with a very fearful adopted dog that had been living in her new forever home with a very nice couple for about three months. The dog showed some signs of improvement but would still not go anywhere near the husband. We put a leash on the dog and started to condition her to the collar and used the leash to have her move towards the husband. We repeated this and over time she learned to move towards the husband without the help of the leash. Once the dog was moving towards the husband we took off the leash. The dog, which had never been within three feet of the husband, now started moving to him. Within a few weeks the collar was off and she now has developed a good relationship with the husband. They go for walks, play, and she is much less stressed.

There are more steps to the process but that is the gist of it. The electronic collar did the job when nothing else could. For me to tell dog owners that they can only use positive reinforcement is the height of unethical and dishonest behavior. To let a dog continue to live in terror because you don't like a particular behavior quadrant is unconscionable. Who really cares about dogs here, the church members or the trainers who are willing to learn how to use the right techniques to help the dog when nothing else can?

Opening an umbrella, using potholders to pick up a hot pan, turning off an alarm clock, applying sunscreen, these are all examples of negative reinforcement. Staying dry and avoiding a cold, keeping your hands from burning, making sure you don't miss work, and preventing sunburn, are all ways negative reinforcement is used. An electronic collar can be used the same way. An E- Collar can be used to stop behavior through punishment, or it can be used to get a behavior to occur through negative reinforcement. The collars today can be set at a level which tingles and is NOT painful. This can be used to teach a dog to come when called.

You can use negative reinforcement to increase the dog's quality of life. This is a positive outcome through negative reinforcement. The come when called command is hands down the most important command to teach your dog. When you are confident that your dog will come back when called, he can run off leash have a much better life than a dog that is always restricted by a leash. Your dog is much safer when he knows to come back to you regardless of distractions. An E-Collar is not always necessary but it can help with this command and others.

Teaching NO with a solid, negative consequence makes the point to the dog to STOP and is one of the most useful words to help you with the recall (come when called). I was working with a little six month old vizsla puppy in Portsmouth, Rhode Island. I had been over the house twice and had taught the puppy the word NO with a negative consequence. It took just two repetitions and this puppy clearly understood the word. On my second visit, a friend of the family stopped by. When the door opened the puppy shot out like a rocket and was tearing around the front yard heading toward the street. The entire family raced out the door and started yelling, *"Come, Come here Penny!"* Penny was having a blast avoiding everyone. I walked out the door and yelled, *"NO!"* She immediately came to a stop, went into a sit position and I was able to walk over and put her on leash.

This would never have been accomplished by all positive, force-free training. Treats meant nothing to Penny in that situation. Here is another clear example of positive reinforcement having its limitations. You see, what most people don't understand is when a dog is running away from you, don't yell COME. Your dog is running AWAY from you. This is a behavior you want to STOP. How do you stop a behavior? Teach the word NO by pairing it with a negative consequence. In this case, I didn't apply the negative consequence because the puppy had already made the association and knew what the word meant. This is also why I say all positive, force-free training is dangerous for your dog. Every problem can't be overcome with a cookie. By teaching the puppy the word NO using a negative consequence the week before, I was able to stop the dog and keep her from running into the street.

So I hope you can see now that avoiding punishment and negative reinforcement is not the best course of action for your dog. I understand the force free, all-positive trainers think they are being nice to their dogs and clients. But avoiding the real world and not understanding behavior and consequences for what they are is not being nice to the dog. The dog who does not know how to stop a behavior, the dog who does not listen to the owner is in danger. Often when training does not work, the dog is confined to the house or a crate or dropped off at the shelter. This is no life for the dog.

Maintaining and promoting the opinion that punishment and negative consequences produce terrible side effects only confuses dog owners. There are side effects to abuse, but when punishment is used the right way, the dog quickly recovers and learns from the experience. Grab a hot pan with a bare hand and there will be side effects. You might get a blister. You may order out for a while, but sooner or later you will go back to using a pan. You won't shrivel in fear or run out the room screaming the next time you see a pan. If you were abused with the same pan, it would be a different story, but burning your hand was a negative consequence (punishment) and it taught you a lesson you will remember to keep you safe in the future.

CHAPTER 7

"You know how advice is. You only want it if it agrees with what you wanted to do anyway."

John Steinbeck

Two Words EVERY Dog Needs To Learn

Teach Your Dog These Two Words And You'll Have The Dog Of Your Dreams

THE BEST PIECE OF DOG TRAINING ADVICE

Did you know that dogs are mentioned forty-four times in the Bible? Cats… zero. There is also some great advice if you're looking for dog training help in the Bible. Here it is:

Proverbs 20:18

"Get good advice and you will succeed." '

Well hot diggity, look at that, dog training guidance from the Good Book. The first three words are key: "*Get good advice,*" because we are constantly given advice and it can be difficult to separate the wheat from the chaff. Take it from a guy who has bumbled around the desert like a lost puppy due to bad advice. I would never give advice on a whole host of subjects, but the one subject I can help you with is dog training.

Why? Because I do not bow down to the politically correct agenda pushing out most of the information you'll find on dog training today. I have zero interest in impressing anyone in my profession. I could care less what the APDT, PPG, or members of the Church of Positive Only Training think of me. And believe me, they no likey The Amazing Dog Training Man. The only thing I am interested in are results and helping you train your dog. Dog training that saves dogs' lives, that helps dogs to become well-behaved, happy members of the family, that's what I'm all about.

The best advice you can ever get is this:
Teach your dog the word YES and teach your dog the word NO.

Teach YES with a positive consequence. With your dog in front of you say the word, "*YES!*" and give a treat. Repeat this over and over until your dog associates the word YES with a positive consequence. You can now use this word to "mark" any behavior you'd like to see more of. SIT, DOWN, STAND, and STAY can be taught using the word YES. This is Classical Conditioning, also referred to as "learning by association". Once your dog understands the word YES you can then use Operant Conditioning, also known as "learning by consequence," to teach all sorts of behaviors.

YES can only be used to teach and reinforce the behaviors you want. It cannot be used to stop or reduce the behaviors that are driving you nuts. This requires using the word NO. When your dog is doing a behavior that is unacceptable you say, "NO!," and pair it with a negative consequence. Once your dog is then doing the acceptable behavior (walking past the meatloaf, keeping all four paws on the ground when greeting) YOU THEN switch back and use positive reinforcement, YES!, and reward your dog for the acceptable behavior. And that, my spiritual friend, is as the Bible states: "Good advice!"

On my website, DeadlyDogTrainingMyth.com, I have a before video of a rottie that went crazy around other dogs. The owners were asked to leave a group obedience class. They called in the Big Dog (that's me) and within two lessons we got him walking within inches of other dogs. I accomplished this through using a combination of YES and NO. The after video shows a happy, well-behaved rottie that is now controllable on leash.

"I Just Want My Dog To Listen To Me!" If I had a dime for every time someone said to me, *"I just want my dog to listen,"* I'd be living in a hundred room mansion on Ocean Drive in Newport, Rhode Island. When you teach your dog both YES and NO, you'll know how to apply positive and negative consequences. Your dog will respond to your commands because you'll be applying the principles of behavior. Once you understand how behavior works, you'll get quick results because you'll be able to communicate effectively with your dog.

INTERSPECIES COMMUNICATION

Have you ever really wanted something for Christmas and didn't get it? My mother-in-law has a great story about a bowling set she got for Christmas when she was a kid. She had told her parents that she wanted "duckpins" for Christmas so they got her exactly what she asked for. Being the good parents they were, they went out and bought a duckpin bowling set. When my mother-in-law opened the gift she was upset and confused and wondered why they got her a bowling set. Later in the day she asked her parents, *"Why did you buy me a bowling set?"* They said: *"Barbie, you said you wanted duckpins."* She then explained to her parents that she wanted the little duck pins that her friend, Joyce, always wore on her shirt collars.

Have you ever see Pulp Fiction? Here is one of my favorite parts of the movie:

Jules: *"You know what they call a Quarter Pounder with cheese in France?"*

Brett: *"No."*

Jules: *"Tell 'em, Vincent."*

Vincent: *"A Royale with cheese."*

Jules: *"A Royale with cheese! You know why they call it that?"*

Brett: "*Because of the metric system?*"

Jules: *"Check out the big brain on Brett! You're a smart..."*

And we'll end the dialogue there. They also don't use the term megabytes in France. Megabytes are called mega-octets. Why am I sharing this with you? Because it's all about CORRECT communication. If I went to France and wanted a Quarter Pounder with cheese I would have to learn the correct word. If I talked about megabytes I would get confused looks. It's up to me to learn how to communicate with people in France.

Remember this with your dog. It is up to YOU to learn how to communicate with your dog. Your dog can learn certain words, but it is up to you to learn how to speak dog. Dogs communicate through body language. You need to pay attention to your dog's tail, ears, hackles, eyes, muzzle, and body. You can easily tell when your dog is happy, his tail is wagging, his ears are back, his body is shaking and it's very easy to know what your dog is communicating to you. Do you also know when your dog is stressed? Nervous? Angry?

It's funny how communication works. And when it comes right down to it, if you're having issues with your dog, I can guarantee that there are communication problems. Having a dog requires leadership, exercise, good nutrition, attention, and most importantly, proper communication. If your dog is not behaving the way you'd like, you are having a communication problem. Throughout this book, I show you how to effectively communicate to your dog so he stops doing behaviors you don't like. You also have to know how to teach your dog to DO behaviors you like. For this to happen, your dog first has to learn the words YES and NO.

When I sit down with a new client I always explain that dogs only do two types of behavior. They do good behaviors and bad behaviors, or to be more accurate, acceptable and unacceptable behaviors. Dogs don't have any concept of right and wrong or morals, so it is more accurate to think in terms of acceptable and unacceptable behaviors. Since your dog only does two types of behaviors, your dog has to learn two words. They must learn YES and they must learn NO. When they learn these two words you can then communicate to your dog what he can and can't do. Throw in a few other words and your dog can understand what you need him to do at any time. I also teach the words GOOD and WRONG. When your dog understands YES, NO, GOOD, and WRONG, you have the skills necessary for interspecies communication. These four words are markers and make it easy for you and your dog to work together.

HOW TO SPEED UP COMMUNICATION

I started training dogs back in 1988 when I was hired to do K9 Security for a large, inner city hospital. I often get strange looks and the follow up question: *"You did K9 security at a hospital?"*

Well, the hospital I worked at was St. Francis Hospital and we were a block and a half away from one of the most dangerous neighborhoods in Hartford, Connecticut. The dogs were one hundred percent a deterrent. Nobody messed with the cars, visitors, and employees at St. Francis. The sight of the dogs walking the grounds was enough of a deterrent to keep the punks at bay.

One funny story I share is when a new CEO was hired from a very safe, small hospital in suburban Ohio. He took one look at the dogs and said, *"Get rid of them. We do not run a Nazi camp here and I will not have German shepherds walking around scaring people."* He did not understand the dogs only scared the people who stole, mugged, and vandalized the hospital. Within one month, the crime on the exterior hospital property skyrocketed. Cars were stolen and broken into, a nurse was mugged one hundred feet from the hospital entrance, and some of the buildings were busted into. Shortly after, a representative from the CEO's office came to the security department and informed us we needed to bring the dogs back. Welcome to the neighborhood!

Anyway, I have always loved dogs so I was very happy to get a job working with them. The thought of doing the training was even more exciting but I was in for a horrible shock the very first week. You see, the training was brutal. Everything was yank and crank. No treats, very little praise, and a lot of corrections with a prong collar. I never felt good about it but what did I know? I was learning from the experts.

I feel fortunate that I was born with a very curious nature. Because the training I was learning did not feel right, I decided to expand my education. What I learned amazed me. I discovered everything we were doing could be approached in a different way with better results. I discovered the principles of operant and classical conditioning, which ALL training is based on. The best way for your dog to learn what they should and should not do is by teaching markers.

Right around this time I get the question: "*Why would I want to use markers to train my dog?*" and sometime followed with: "*Must I use them to train my dog?*"

FIRST - You absolutely do NOT have to use markers. I have trained boatloads of dogs without them. So the question is... why recommend them? Markers are used for one MAIN REASON: They speed up the training process! Nothing works quicker than a marker and nothing is as effective as marker training. Remember, training is communication. We want to teach our dogs to DO certain behaviors and we want our dogs to STOP doing other ones.

The words YES and NO are both markers. YES is associated with a positive consequence and NO with a negative one. Once your dog learns those two words, you can communicate to him that you either want more of a behavior to occur, or you want a behavior to stop. Remember, when you want your dog to do a behavior for you, use a positive consequence. When you want your dog to STOP doing a behavior, use a negative consequence. The marker and reward (or punishment) will help your dog learn much faster than any other method because there is no confusion.

ASSOCIATIONS AND CONSEQUENCES

Learning happens through repetition, or as they say in Latin, "*Repetitio mater studiorum est.*" Repetition is the mother of all learning. Sometimes learning can happen within a few repetitions. Other times it may take hundreds of repetitions. Dogs learn two ways. They will learn through associations and consequences. Learning through association occurs all the time. If you open the refrigerator door and your dog walks over and you hand him a slice of cheese, your dog will start to associate the sound of the fridge door opening with getting a slice of cheese. A few more repetitions and your dog will come running from the other room when he hears the door open. You also see this happen with a cat that is fed canned food. He hears the sound of the can opener and sure enough, the cat comes running. This is also known as classical conditioning, just think of Ole Pavlov and his dogs with the bell.

The second way a dog learns is by consequence. You call your dog over and ask him to sit. He sits and you give him a treat. The consequence for sitting was the treat. Positive reinforcement was used to make the behavior stronger and more likely to occur in the future. This is learning through consequence, also known as operant conditioning. To train your dog, you'll use a combination of learning through association and consequence. Remember, consequences can be positive or negative.

CLASSICAL CONDITIONING

In 1849 in Ryazan, Russia, the village priest and his wife gave birth to a son. This boy, Ivan, would go on to become a Nobel Peace Prize winner and change the way the world looks at behavior. Ivan Pavlov devoted his life to science and his studies lead to the development of Classical Conditioning, and this is VERY important for dog owners. Many people are familiar with Pavlov's dogs. He ran experiments in which he rang a bell and then sent meat powder through tubes into the dogs' mouths. After repeating this a few times, the dogs would begin to salivate every time they heard the bell. In 1901, he termed this response a conditioned reflex. A conditioned reflex is a learned behavior, one that happens in response to a stimulus.

So let me explain why this is so important for you. Your dog is constantly developing conditioned reflexes that can affect his behavior. For example, a lot of dogs go bananas when someone rings the bell or knocks on the door. This is a conditioned reflex. It was classically conditioned and once you understand this, you can use it to change your dog's behavior. We are going to use classical conditioning (learning through association) to teach your dog the words YES and NO.

OPERANT CONDITIONING

We have our old friend B.F. Skinner to thank for showing us how dogs learn through consequences. The good professor is the one who coined the term, Operant Conditioning. Operant conditioning is a way of learning through rewards and punishments. An example often used is rats who were put into an operant conditioning chamber, sometimes referred to as a Skinner Box. Inside the box were two different levers. One lever was red and would electrify the little critter every time he touched it. The other lever was blue and would release a food pellet when pressed. The rat learned to avoid the red lever and push the blue one. Skinner and his crew worked mostly with rats and pigeons to see how different reward and punishment schedules influenced how often the levers were pushed. When you are training your dog, you'll use operant conditioning to strengthen or reduce behaviors.

A REAL LIFE STORY

Let's start with a story of my friend who did not want my help training his dog. I've changed the names to protect the innocent so we'll just refer to him as Fred. This happens a lot. Friends and family members are not impressed that I am a highly-skilled dog training specialist. Over twelve million views of my videos on YouTube, thousands of email subscribers, two books on Amazon, and they think I am just some schlep when it comes to dog training. Amusing.

Anyway... Fred bought a three-month-old puppy from a breeder. He always wanted a boxer and was happy as a clam with his new pup. He called me up one morning and asked if I wanted to go to the beach and let our dogs run around. *"Sure,"* I said and went to meet him and his new boxer pup.

It was a great day. The sun was out, there was a gentle breeze blowing in from Buzzards Bay, and not too many people around so the dogs could run and play. We spent about an hour there and then it was time to go. Fred's puppy had been having a blast, running, splashing in the waves, rolling in dead fish, typical boxer puppy antics. As we were getting ready to go, Fred looked at his pup and called, *"COME!"*

I knew what was going to happen. Fred didn't know it, but he was about to make a HUGE training mistake, so I said, *"Fred, can I give you some advice when it comes to calling your pup to you?"*

"Naw, look at him. He's doing great, he's coming right to me." And his little boxer pup did race to him. It would have made a great Puppy Chow commercial. This adorable boxer puppy with his ears back, eyes smiling, face beaming, sun shining, waves crashing in the background was racing right to Fred.

Once his pup got close, Fred reached in his back pocket, took out his leash and… clipped the leash on his collar. In a split second he made the cardinal sin of recalls. You see, he just punished his dog for coming when called. Sure enough, within a few weeks, Fred was having major problems getting his now bigger, older, more confident boxer pup back on leash.

So let's back up a second. That first day at the beach, Fred applied what is called negative punishment. Negative punishment is when something is taken away. This is what Fred did to his puppy. He took away his freedom. He UNINTENTIONALLY used negative punishment and now had a problem teaching his puppy to come back to him. This is why I always take a little time to teach the four behavior quadrants to new clients. If you do not understand them, you may be doing something unintentionally that is hurting your training and then wondering why you are not getting the results you should.

I also want to make it clear when you want your dog to DO a behavior for you i.e. SIT, DOWN, STAND, STAY, etc., you use the R+ quadrant - positive reinforcement. When you want your dog to STOP doing a behavior you have a choice of the two quadrants, +P or P-, positive punishment or negative punishment.

So let's break down the four behavior quadrants so you have a clear understanding moving forward.

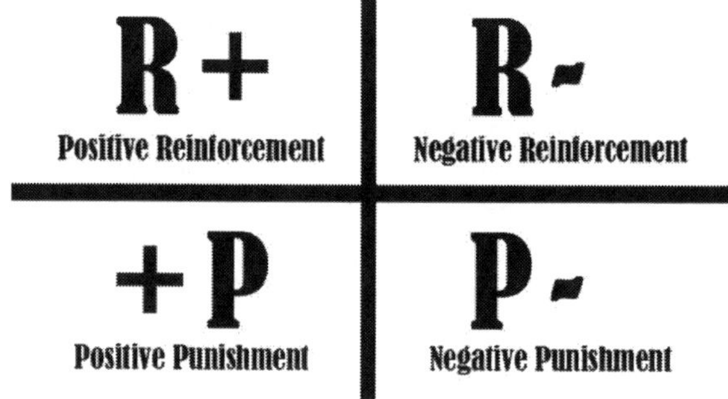

R+ (Positive Reinforcement) - This is the quadrant we use to teach behaviors. SIT, DOWN, STAND, COME, and LOOSE LEASH WALKING are taught by rewarding the behavior with something your dog likes: treats, toys, praise, etc. By definition, positive reinforcement can NOT be used to STOP behaviors.

R- (Negative Reinforcement) - This quadrant is also used to teach behaviors. The old style of training often relied on negative reinforcement. A common way to teach SIT using R- is with a choke chain. The leash was lifted and the choke chain was tightened around the dog's neck until he sat. The pressure from the leash (R-) does not stop until the dog does the desire command. Negative reinforcement can also be used in a way that does not inflict pain, which is important to remember.

+P (Positive Punishment) - This is the quadrant used to stop behaviors. When your dog does any behavior you want to stop, you'll be using positive punishment. A clear verbal command, NO, is given and then followed up with a negative consequence, putting an end to the undesired behavior. Please remember what I said earlier - this does not mean any pain will be inflicted on your dog, just a negative consequence.

P- (Negative Punishment) - This quadrant is also used to stop behaviors. Negative punishment is when you take something away from the dog, something the dog wants. My friend, Fred, used negative punishment that day on the beach. His little boxer wanted to continue playing. By putting him on leash, he took his pup's freedom away and made a very clear association with coming when called - stay away, humans end all fun.

To wrap this up before moving on, your dog has to learn the word YES so you can communicate to him that he has just done the correct behavior. YES is paired with a positive consequence like food to help strengthen the behavior. Your dog also has to learn the word NO. When he understands the word NO, you can communicate to your dog that he has just done an unacceptable behavior. The word NO is paired with a negative consequence to reduce or eliminate the behavior.

CHAPTER 8

"Properly used, positive reinforcement is extremely powerful."

B. F. Skinner

Good quote but ole B.F. forgot to add three words... "*to teach behavior.*"

How To Teach Your Dog "YES"

Using Positive Reinforcement To Teach Your Dog

It was July 1945, and a world weary of war was waiting to hear what Japanese Premier, Kantaro Suzuki, was going to do about the Potsdam Declaration. Would he agree to the terms that called for the surrender of the Japanese Armed Forces? Trying to be careful with his choice of words, he stated that his cabinet was adopting a position of mokusatzu. And that one word, "mokusatzu," sealed the fate of hundreds of thousands of Japanese citizens.

That one word lead to the bombing of Hiroshima and Nagasaki. You see, the word mokusatzu has two meanings. It can mean "without comment for the moment" or it can mean "ignore." The Japanese News Agency mistakenly translated the word as "ignore" and when the news made its way to President Truman, he decided there was no other course of action but to drop the atomic bomb. Tragic.

Communication. How much in life is about communication? Say the right word at the right time and amazing things can happen. Say one wrong word at the wrong time and over two hundred thousand people lose their lives. And that was among the same species, different languages, but all humans involved. Imagine how hard our dogs have it trying to understand us. This is why you have to make sure you are clearly communicating to your dog. The best way is to use a system of markers that lets your dog know when he has done something correctly, when he needs to try again, and when to stop doing something.

It all starts with classical conditioning. You pair a word or sound with something your dog likes or finds unpleasant, depending on whether you want to increase or decrease behavior. In addition to YES and NO, I also teach the words GOOD, WRONG, and BREAK. WRONG is to let your dog know he made a mistake and GOOD is verbal feedback to keep going. GOOD is for duration and multiple commands. We'll get into using and teaching those words in just a moment. Once your dog understands the word YES means reward, you can start to use it for teaching behaviors. For example, as you say the command SIT, you will "mark" the behavior just as your dog is doing it. So as soon as your dog's butt hits the deck, say YES and deliver the reward. If you have taught your dog the word YES, he will understand what the reward was for.

TEACHING THE WORD YES

Pairing the word YES with a reward is how you give the word value to your dog. Right now, the word means nothing. If you just keep saying the word YES without connecting it to something of value, there is no communication. So, you start associating the word with a treat. In the beginning, what you are doing is called classical conditioning, or learning through association. You want the word YES to have meaning the same way the sound of the refrigerator door opening does. The best way to start teaching this is with your dog and a bag of high value treats. Say your dog's name and then say YES enthusiastically. The second after you say YES, give your dog a treat. Repeat this two hundred times and the word will start to take on a meaning. The word YES will have value. You can test the word by waiting for your dog to lie down and relax. Once he is lying there, say the word YES and wait to see if he turns his head. If he turns and looks, you know that your dog now understands the word. This is great. You have a word to use that lets your dog know when he has done a behavior you want. From this point forward, you can say YES the second your dog does a behavior like SIT, DOWN, STAY, or even when they urinate outside if you are housetraining.

A high value reward, usually some kind of yummy treat, associated with the word YES is the way your dog is going to learn his obedience. When you start teaching this word you can use small tiny little pieces of the treat. The quantity of treats used to teach YES is high so small pieces are the way to go. Hot dogs work great because they are soft and can be cut into little tiny bits. You can use half a hot dog and chop it up into fifty little pieces. Another way I teach this is by using the dog's regular food that you put into a bowl every day. Instead of putting the food into a bowl, put the same amount of your dog's food into a little baggie and leave it on the counter. This way throughout the day you can tell your dog YES and hand him a kibble. By using your dog's regular food you can do repeated pairings of the word YES and food throughout the day. By the end of one week you'll have logged hundreds of repetitions. Once the word is paired it is a very powerful way to communicate to your dog what you want him to do. Once he figures out the meaning of the word, you clear up confusion and your timing will be much better.

Training is all about your dog understanding what is expected of him. Using the word YES paired with a reward drastically improves your timing and speeds up the whole training process. I have seen dogs learn three behaviors as one because of poor timing. If you give your dog the command SIT, there is a chance that your dog will sit and then he might sniff the air, bark, and try to give paw. By the time your reward reaches him, he may think he has been rewarded for sitting, giving paw, sniffing the air, and barking. If this happens often enough, when you tell him SIT, you'll automatically get all of those behaviors instead of just the sit. This is why markers are so handy. They give the correct information to your dog when he has done the specific behavior you want.

A whistle is a marker and is often used at places like SeaWorld to train dolphins and killer whales. If you've ever been to a show, you'll see them using the whistle and delivering fish. So to train a killer whale, you blow the whistle and toss a fish. This is done over and over (classical conditioning) to give the sound of the whistle meaning to the whale. Once it understands that the whistle means fish, they are off to the races with the training. The trainers can communicate from a distance to the whale when it has done the correct behavior. When the dolphin is on the other side of the pool and jumps through a hoop, the trainer can blow the whistle the second the dolphin makes the jump. The dolphin can be fifty feet away but still understand it did the correct behavior and can come back to the trainer to get the fish. So, once the whistle has been classically conditioned (the marine mammals understand that a whistle means fish) the trainer can then communicate to them when they do correct behavior (which is operant conditioning).

What's important to remember when comparing dog training to marine mammal training is that the marine mammals are contained and do not have the same options as your dog. A dolphin's tank is a highly controlled environment. Your dog, when off leash, is not in a controlled environment and that is why you need both positive and negative consequences.

WHAT IF YOUR DOG DOESN'T LIKE TREATS

Dolphin trainers will often use deprivation to get behaviors. I have clients that tell me their dogs do not have very good appetites and are not interested in treats. My answer is simple. Take the food away and wait twenty-four hours. After a day of no food, most dogs will start eating. It's funny when they tell me they could never do that to their dogs. I laugh because the dogs weren't eating anyway. So what's the problem with taking the food up for a day and helping the dog develop an appetite? This way once the dog is interested and wants to eat, you can use that to your advantage to train. A dog in the wild will often go for days without eating and most dogs will be fine.

You must also look at the type of treats you are using. Some dogs will scarf down anything put in front of them. Others will hold out for the good stuff. Most dog biscuits are made from grains and are not very appealing. Something soft, like a hot dog, can make the difference between a dog that will work for food and one that won't. It is also difficult to train a dog using food if he has access to his bowl all day, because a dog that always has access to the food bowl won't be motivated to work for food.

OTHER REWARDS PAIRED WITH YES

YES can be associated with rewards other than treats. In the beginning, it's best to use treats to teach YES, but once your dog starts to get it you can use other rewards. Let's say your dog is a ball nut. He goes out of his mind for the ball. You can ask for a SIT. Once your dog is in the sit position you would say YES and then toss the ball. You can do this with your dog's freedom, the leash, the door and anything else your dog loves. Once your dog understands the SIT command, the word YES is a release from the command because he has completed it successfully and your dog gets his freedom back. The freedom is the reward. If your dog gets excited walking through the door, make your dog sit and before you open the door, have your dog stay. Open the door and then say YES and let your dog walk through. It is good to associate other rewards with the word YES once your dog has an understanding of the meaning.

ONCE YOU SAY YES, THE BEHAVIOR IS OVER

The biggest mistake I see when using the word YES as a marker is repeating it over and over. Repeating the word will not help communicate to your dog. When your dog does the command, say YES once and give the reward. The behavior is completed. It is common for dog owners to say "*YES, YES, YES,*" when the dog has done a behavior. There is no reason to repeat the word. If you are doing multiple commands with your dog use GOOD in between. So if you said SIT, DOWN, SIT, PAW, you would not say YES after each command. Instead, you will start using the word GOOD for some verbal feedback. So I often will say SIT, GOOD, DOWN, GOOD, SIT, GOOD, PAW, YES and then give the reward. GOOD is used to keep the dog going.

TEACHING THE WORD GOOD

GOOD is the word you'll use to communicate to your dog that he is doing the command correctly and to keep doing it. So if your dog is doing a stay, you would say, GOOD, GOOD, and at the end of the stay command you would say YES and deliver a treat. Remember, when you say YES, the command is completed. Your dog has been told that he did a good job and is done with the command.

So the word GOOD is way to communicate to your dog that he is doing the right thing and to keep on doing it. I like to let the dog know that I am pleased with him. So, I'll often say GOOOD, GOOOOOOD, GOOOOOOOD

SPARKY! GOOD is paired with verbal praise, not a treat. The treat is saved for when the command is completed with the word YES.

TEACHING THE WORD WRONG

Another word that I teach and use early in training is the word WRONG. This is a great word because in the early stages of training your dog is going to make mistakes. If you started dog training when I did, you would be familiar with the old style "yank and crank" method. When the dog made a mistake, instead of helping the dog learn a leash correction would be given. This led to HUGE problems - everything from the dog becoming inhibited to fearful to aggressive. And once the dog was labeled aggressive, it was usually a short, one-way ride to the vet. The problem was created because of the training. Poor communication (training) and the dog pays for it. Tragic.

In the early stages of training, you do NOT want to apply any kind of correction. Giving your dog a correction too early in training will result in your dog getting nervous and you may suppress your dog's willingness to perform the commands. But when your dog does not perform the command, you do not want to keep repeating it. You want to let your dog know he made a mistake without hurting his performance. When your dog does not complete the command, you are going to simply say WRONG and turn away from him.

It's a good thing I didn't go to high school in 2016 because when I was in high school I was always one step away from getting tossed out. I never quite fit in and was labeled with a learning problem which often resulted in frustration, frustration for the teachers and me. I made a lot of mistakes which some teachers thought were intentional. Since school was so dreadful, I often took the liberty to skip certain classes. I also choose to skip whole days of school. I spent many hours in detention. I was also suspended a lot which was really terrible because it was in-school suspension.

I know, hard to believe but one hundred percent true. In my junior year the Vice Principal said to me, *"Congratulations Letendre. You're in first place."* First place for what? I thought. *"You're in first place for most detentions,"* he clarified. Great.

Making mistakes is a big part of learning. You'll make mistakes while you are training your dog and your dog will make mistakes while trying to learn English from you. So, one of the best words to teach your dog is... WRONG.

If you don't use the word WRONG, there's a good chance you'll give your dog a reward for doing an incomplete command. With many dogs, if you ask for a DOWN, they'll go three quarters of the way to floor. If your dog gets the reward, you have just made a mistake because you did not ask for a three quarter down. If you want your dog to go all the way down you have to reward for the correct behavior. Another trap a lot of dog owners fall into is repeating the command if it's not performed the first time. I've heard plenty of dog owners say, *"Sparky down, lie down. DOWN! I SAID LIE DOWN RIGHT NOW! SPARKY DOOWWWNNN!!!"*

So to avoid these mistakes, start using the word WRONG and reward only for correct behavior. Also, say the command one time. Here's how to do it. Call your dog over and say SIT. If he immediately sits, say YES and reward. If your dog does anything else, if he backs up, if he barks at you, if he goes into a down, if he gives a paw, simply withhold the reward, say WRONG and turn away from him for a moment. After a second or two face your dog and say SIT again. If he sits, quickly say YES and reward. Anything else... WRONG and turn away.

This is a great word and it will help clear up the confusion between you and your dog while training. Often when a dog does not perform a command it is because he is confused, distracted, or not motivated. After you turn away from your dog, you'll get him engaged and his attention back on you to try again. It is important to remember that your dog ONLY gets the reward when the command is done correctly.

TEACHING THE WORD BREAK

BREAK is the word we use to let the dog know the exercise is completed. It is important for your dog to learn from the start to hold the command until you release. For example: You ask for a SIT. Most dogs would do the SIT command and once they do it, they get up and move on. You want your dog to learn to hold the SIT until you release, much like the STAY command. Your dog will learn to do STAY until you say, "BREAK!" BREAK is the all-clear signal. You can get up now. This is very important for your dog to learn. If you ask for a SIT as your friend walks into your house, you want your dog to stay sitting until you release. Otherwise, your dog could bolt out the door or jump on your friend. As you teach commands, you'll reward your dog and once you decide it's long enough, you'll say, "BREAK!"

WHAT ABOUT CLICKERS

Clickers have become very popular since the nineties. Clickers are an excellent way to teach your dog commands. A clicker is a small box with a metal strip that makes a very distinct sound when you push it down. The click is associated with the treats and it is conditioned the same way as the word YES. You can find them in most any pet store.

You may be wondering why I teach YES instead of using a clicker because they actually do work better. They produce such a distinct sound your dog gets conditioned to the clicker much faster than your voice. I just know from experience though, that clickers are often confusing to dog owners. It is also one extra thing to have in your hands on top of the treats and the leash while training, and you might lose it or forget it at home, or forget it in the car. You always have your voice and the word YES doesn't take an extra hand during a training session, so, that's why I choose to use the word YES. If you prefer to use a clicker, it would replace the word YES in your training. The clicker communicates to your dog he has just completed the correct behavior.

A lot of people also think they must always use a clicker in order to get the dog to do behaviors but that's not necessary. Once your dog learns the behavior, you can reward your dog without the clicker. But if you use a clicker while you are first teaching a command, it will greatly speed up the training process.

CAN I TRAIN WITHOUT MAKERS?

Remember that confusion is what you are always trying to avoid when training your dog. I often get asked if dogs can be trained without the use of markers. You can train without markers but in my humble but accurate opinion, the best and most effective way to communicate to your dog is through markers. The marker will let your dog know what he is doing right, what he is doing wrong, what he should continue doing, and what he needs to stop doing.

So the words or markers we use in dog training are YES, NO, GOOD and WRONG. YES is paired with a positive consequence and used to TEACH behaviors. NO is paired with a negative consequence and used to STOP behaviors. GOOD is paired with verbal praise and used for duration to KEEP your dog doing behaviors. WRONG is paired with the removal of the treat and attention to let your dog know he made a MISTAKE and to try again. It really is a lot of fun to train this way once you get the hang of it. You can train without the use of markers. I did for years, but once I started using them I was hooked because I could see the improved results.

Now in the next chapter we will be teaching what you've all been waiting for. You'll learn how to teach the word NO to get your dog to STOP doing behaviors.

CHAPTER 9

"Saying NO can be the ultimate self-care."

Claudia Black

"Saying NO can be the ultimate dog care."

Eric Letendre

How To Teach Your Dog "NO"

Here It Is! The Chapter You've Been Waiting For
Learn How To STOP Behavior

Answer this question: Your dog bolts through the front door and takes off. How do you get your dog to come back to you? Most people would take off after their dogs and yell, *"COME!!!!!"* and have some kind of treat ready. A lot of trainers will tell you to just offer a treat and your dog will come back. If only it were that easy. The problem with this advice is that it places positive reinforcement on a mantle, gives the illusion it can solve all your problems. WRONG! Your dog is free, your dog is looking for action. The positive reinforcement of being free is STRONGER than whatever treat you are offering. You know that your dog often ignores your treats, that he is much more interested in exploring the big, exciting world that lies beyond the front door. Sure, there are some dogs out there that will come back for a treat but the vast majority won't. So, what do you do if your dog does not want the treat you are offering? If your dog is running away from you or does not want your treat, hopefully your dog has a clear understanding of the word NO.

I traveled up to Rockland, MA to help a dog that was on his way back to the shelter. One of his big problems was refusing to come back to the owners when he was let out into his fenced-in yard. The owner told me he had recently spent up to an hour chasing his dog around the backyard. So we spent the majority of the lesson teaching the word NO. Before it was time to leave, I asked if we could go outside. We let the dog run around for a few minutes and then I asked the owner to call his dog. The dog did what was expected. He immediately went into a play bow, his butt up in the air, tail wagging with the "Come and try and catch me" look. I asked the owner to show me what he normally does to get his dog back. He offered food, he called, he threatened, and even tried to chase him down.

I explained to him that when a dog is doing a behavior we want to STOP, we have to use the word NO, which we had just taught him inside the house a little earlier. A dog running away is doing a behavior we want to STOP. Once the dog stops, we can give him the command we want: COME. I then demonstrated. I said the dog's name and clearly, firmly said, NO! The dog hit the brakes. I then said COME. He trotted over to me and I said YES and rewarded him with a treat.

NO is important to teach your dog because he is always going to only do two types of behavior. He is going to do behaviors you like (SIT, DOWN, STAY, etc.) and behaviors you don't like (running away, chewing, jumping, etc.). This is why your dog needs to learn YES and NO. YES is taught with a positive consequence. NO is taught with a negative consequence. YES is used to reinforce and reward behaviors we like and want more of. NO is used to reduce or eliminate a behavior we don't like. I have spent enough time proving that punishment and negative consequences are NOT abuse. It is NOT mean or unscientific. Now in this chapter, you can learn exactly how I teach a dog NO to STOP unwanted behaviors.

UNDERSTANDING PUNISHMENT

Scarlett, my three-year-old daughter, loves to help. Anytime I am doing anything she'll jump right in and try her best. One place she especially loves to get involved is the kitchen. Normally, I think this is great, but it also makes me nervous when there are sharp knives and boiling pots of water being used. I don't want to discourage her helping nature and curiosity, but sometimes it's necessary she leave the area, so how did I solve this problem? I used punishment. I figured out how to use punishment to get little Scarlett to leave the kitchen. When I want Scarlett to leave the kitchen for her own safety I say five words. *"Time to chop the onions."* She hears those five words and off she goes, no fuss or the need to ask her more than once. She associates onions with an unpleasant experience and to avoid the smell she leaves the room.

This is a form of punishment. The church members have distorted punishment so much by always linking it to abuse but nothing could be further from the truth. And every time I say I am chopping an onion, I make sure to take one out and chop it up. Scarlett was never physically touched, never harmed in any way, but by using something she finds unpleasant, I was able to change her behavior.

A friend of mine told me when he was in high school and had friends over they always behaved. They would go into the basement and never turned the music up loud, no one got drunk, and they never got too rowdy. The reason? It wasn't the threat of his father coming downstairs and yelling at him. He wasn't even concerned about his father coming down and beating him, which he never did. Instead, he was petrified of his father coming to the basement in his tightie whities. The thought of his father walking downstairs in his underwear in front of his friends was enough for him to behave.

ACCOUNTING FOR STRESS

Stress is why the church members freak out when it comes to using a negative consequence. I'll be honest with you, when you use a negative consequence you will put stress on the dog, unless you're working with a black lab. I am convinced they are incapable of feeling any stress. Just kidding. Anyone who tells you a negative consequence does not put pressure on your dog is lying. What you must understand is there are two types of stress. There is chronic stress and acute stress.

Chronic stress is not good. It is unhealthy and dangerous for humans and dogs. Chronic stress is brought on by unending, unyielding, long-term exposure to stressors. A dog under the constant threat of punishment does suffer. A dog wearing an electronic collar with an owner who thinks he can just push a button to get the dog to behave is under chronic stress. This is a terrible situation and it unfortunately happens. I've seen it, and in the wrong hands, electronic collars can be a disaster for dogs. This kind of long-term stress can result in aggression and other psychological problems.

Acute stress is different. Acute stress is what we experience on a more regular basis. Acute stress can be experienced when you are late for work or have a deadline. It can also bring some excitement into your life. Skydiving, scuba diving, or riding a roller coaster can bring on acute stress. Without a little stress in our lives, things would get boring pretty fast.

As I write this, my wife and mother-in-law are experiencing acute stress. They just found a mouse caught between the sliding screen door and the sliding glass door. The poor little field mouse can't do anything to either one of them. He'd have to break the glass to come after them, which would never happen, but the sight of the mouse caught between the screen and glass door has them flipping out. Being the brave husband, I decided to help the little mouse on his way. As I approached the door, they both screamed and asked me to what I was going to do. I found a small stick and with it I helped guide the little guy out from between the doors and off into the woods he ran. With the mouse gone, normal morning routines resumed. Stress was gone and breakfast was made and life continued on. This is a perfect example of acute stress. As I sit here writing and watching this whole thing play out, I can obviously see there are no long-term side effects. They are not breaking down into tears, melting into puddles on the floor, or becoming aggressive towards me.

The force-free, all positive crowd thinks your dog should never experience ANY stress, but stress is part of life and helps you deal with experiences as they come along. Acute stress transpires over a short period of time. When you apply a negative consequence to teach your dog to STOP doing a behavior, it happens in a split second. And as you'll see, as soon as the dog understands what is expected of him, the stress is taken away by switching to positive reinforcement when he gives you the correct behavior.

NEGATIVE CONSEQUENCES

We use a negative consequence to stop behaviors. This is also known as punishment. When I discuss using negative consequences, everyone always asks me what exactly that negative consequence is. Only your dog can answer that question. It could be a squirt of water. It could be a stern voice if you have a sensitive dog, or it could be an electronic collar. My in-law's Cavalier King Charles Spaniel is very sensitive. You can use a squirt bottle to get him to stop a behavior. So to teach him NO, I made sure when he started to do a behavior that was unacceptable, I said NO and then applied a squirt from the bottle. Nothing harsh, but it got my point across. For a lot of dogs, the squirt bottle tends to work for a little while, and then you need to up your game. When you apply a negative consequence, it should stop the behavior within a few repetitions. If you must keep applying it, then the consequence is not right for the dog. It's interesting that a dog can learn the word NO within a few repetitions while learning YES can take hundreds of reps. We do tend to learn faster from avoiding than from gaining.

Temperament always plays a role when it comes to punishment. You can evaluate a dog's temperament on a one to ten scale of soft to hard, one being a soft dog, ten being one physically and mentally tough dog. I had a Great Dane and a Belgian malinois at the same time. The Great Dane was a one and the malinois was a ten. The Great Dane was a huge mush and no negative consequence was even needed with him. If you raised your voice he would stop what he was doing and go lie down. My wife could walk him off leash around downtown Newport with zero problems. She could walk past out of control dogs, on busy sidewalks, and right into the stores. He would stay glued to her side and do whatever was asked of him. My malinois was a different story. He was tough as nails and would always test to see what he could get away with. A raised voice meant nothing to him. So when it comes to teaching your dog NO, it may require you to be a certain way with one dog and different with another depending on their temperaments. In my experience, I find the majority of dogs fall somewhere in the middle. A good, solid, negative consequence is needed to get your point across and teach the dog to stop doing whatever behavior you might find unacceptable.

HOW TO TEACH NO

Sequence is important when you are teaching your dog the word NO with an unpleasant consequence. This may seem like a trivial point but if you don't follow the directions I outline here, your dog will never learn. When you teach NO, you always have to give a warning. Say the word NO first, and then apply the consequence. If you do it the other way around, your dog will never learn. So you must say NO and then apply the consequence.

Imagine if you were standing with your back to me and I had a stick in my hands. I swing the stick and whack your arm with it. After I whack your head, I yell DUCK. We repeat. I swing and WHACK. Then I yell DUCK. You would get upset pretty quickly. Now let's make one small minor but major adjustment. This time I yell DUCK and then I swing the stick. You would only get whacked once. When I yell DUCK and swing the stick again, you would duck to avoid the punishment of the stick. You'd learn to change your behavior to avoid an unpleasant consequence.

Another good example is a caution sign alerting you to a curvy road up ahead. It gives you a chance to change your behavior (slow down and pay more attention) to avoid a wreck. See how this punishment stuff saves lives? This is why I point to the force-free, all positive crowd and say what they preach is dangerous. Without the warning sign on the road, you could suffer some negative consequences.

Warning your dog and teaching him to avoid certain behaviors makes your dog much safer. An Invisible Fence gives a warning which prevents your dog from leaving the yard and getting crushed by a thousand pounds of moving steel on wheels. A warning taught with a negative consequence can prevent your dog from eating a chicken bone out of the garbage. When your dog has learned to avoid a negative consequence and keeps all four paws on the ground when greeting, he won't jump and scratch Aunt Martha who's on a blood thinning drug.

DIFFERENT WAYS TO APPLY A NEGATIVE CONSEQUENCE

I hope I made the point punishment does not have to hurt or inflict pain on your dog. What I have learned over the years is pain is NOT a good way to apply a negative consequence. Dogs have an incredibly high pain threshold and can withstand an enormous amount of pain. As predatory animals, they are able to take quite a pounding. Hunting prey larger than themselves takes a toll on their bodies. They get kicked, bitten, and knocked around.

The dog's startle reflex, however, is much more sensitive which makes the negative consequence of choice for me, the bonker. A bonker is nothing more than a rolled up towel held together with two elastic bands. When you bonk a dog, his startle reflex makes it unpleasant, and you can stop a behavior in its tracks. I like the bonker for many reasons. It does not cost you any money and it does not inflict any pain on the dog. Let's say your dog likes to jump on you. As your dog jumps, say NO and then apply a good bonk to your dog. Yes, literally bonk your dog in the head with the rolled up towel. This technique will not hurt your dog and does not require any fancy equipment. I know it's not as sexy as a fancy electronic collar, but in most cases it works better.

WHO IS GARY WILKES?

The Association of Professional Dog Trainers holds an annual conference every year. In 1996, I went to their third annual conference in Phoenix, Arizona. While there, I attended a talk discussing aversive control given by a trainer named Gary Wilkes. During his talk, he showed how to teach boundaries. He did it with humans and silly string. He never told the humans in his demonstration what they were going to learn. He gave them a warning (NO) and then squirted the participants with the silly string. He trained them to not pass a threshold using a warning and the silly string as the only forms of communication. At the end, he asked the participants what he was teaching them. They all agreed they were learning to not cross a boundary. It was one of the best talks I have ever seen and still remember it all these years later.

Gary Wilkes is one of the most ethical trainers on the planet. He, along with Karen Pryor, introduced clickers to the dog training world through a series of seminars they held together in 1992 and 1993. But Gary always believed you must also use aversive control to stop behavior and has never backed away from this position. He has helped save countless dogs' lives by teaching others how to correctly use punishment to stop behaviors. As the mass movement of all positive grew, he did not cave to their flawed, force-free ideology and from what I understand, he has been attacked by church members and un-invited to speak at different events.

Gary Wilkes taught me how to use the bonker and deserves all the credit for this ingenious technique to STOP behavior. Thanks to Gary and the information he shares, I have been able to help thousands of dogs and their families and we all owe him a huge debt of gratitude for his work with dogs and his contributions to the dog training profession. If you'd like to see him demonstrate the use of a bonker, please visit his YouTube channel: YouTube.com/wilkesgm1

NEGATIVE CONSEQUENCES DO APPLY PRESSURE

Since pressure is applied with a negative consequence, you need to switch back to positive reinforcement and reward your dog when the correct behavior occurs. Let's take jumping again. When I am dealing with a dog that is jumping, I say NO and then bonk the dog. I then invite him back up. If he jumps again, I reapply the bonk. I repeat this process. At this point, most people start to freak out because I keep inviting the dog back up. I do this for a couple of reasons. First, I want to make sure if anyone does come over your house and invites your dog up, he will look at as a cue to keep his paws on the floor. Second, I always want to bring the dog to a place where I can reward his behavior. So after I invite the dog to jump and he keeps all four feet on the deck, I mark the behavior, YES (remember last chapter) and deliver a reward. I also make a big deal out it when the dog gives me the correct behavior. I often think of the line from the Godfather, *"It's not personal, just business."* I then praise the dog and play with him for a few seconds. I do everything I can to take away the stress from the correction and let the dog know he has done the correct behavior.

In most cases, I can stop jumping in about five minutes. How many people live with dogs that must be crated or put outside every time someone comes over the house? How many dogs are confined and not allowed to socialize with human guests because they can't behave? They are often banned to crates or bedrooms when someone comes over for years when just a little bit of punishment could teach the dog to stop jumping. It still boggles my mind that church members can't see this.

WHAT ABOUT ELECTRONIC COLLARS?

Electronic collars have become extremely popular. Whenever the topic of punishment or negative consequences is broached, this comes up. Electronic collars can be very effective and the technology has become so much more refined. Anytime you are punishing behaviors you must make sure there is some consistency.

A client of mine has grandchildren. Every time they come over, her chocolate lab steals food from them. It has become irritating to her and she wants it to stop. She asked me about getting an electronic collar. I told her the collar could fix the food stealing but here's the problem. First, if she was going to use it, she needed to make sure she was there to catch her dog every time she attempted to steal the food until the behavior was eliminated. Next, if the kids fed her when no one was looking, it really wouldn't be fair to the dog if she is given a negative consequence later on for the same behavior.

So, yes, an electronic collar can be used to stop this behavior. You just want to make sure you are using it the right way. Collars available today have many more settings than the old versions. This is good because you can set them to the precise level you need to get your point across to your dog.

WHY ELECTRONIC FENCES WORK SO WELL

Consistency is one the reasons Invisible Fence works so well. There is no human component. There is no one there to apply the consequence. It is done automatically. If the owner had to be there to teach the boundaries, there would be inconsistencies. When you are training you must be sure you are as consistent as possible. When it comes to punishing a behavior, you must keep your head on a swivel to make sure the information you're giving your dog stays consistent.

When I discuss underground containment systems or E-Collars, it is important to understand there are different brands and there are shoddy products out there. If you are going to purchase a containment system or E-Collar, make sure you get a quality product. You should also get some instruction from a qualified dog trainer. There is no doubt that E-Collars can be great training devices, but at the same time, they can be the worst. This does not mean we should get rid of them, ban them, or outlaw them as they have done in parts of Australia and England. You just must use them correctly, much like a surgeon's scalpel, which can be used to slash someone open or to provide a lifesaving operation.

WHAT ABOUT PRONG COLLARS?

Prong collars generate almost as much controversy as E-Collars. The prong collar is often misunderstood because of its appearance. A quick glance and you can see why people freak out over them. They look like a torture device from a Quentin Tarantino movie. A quick search on Google or Facebook will show you terrible pictures of them imbedded in dogs' necks and talk of having them sharpened to get a better response from the dog. Again, anyone who would sharpen one to inflict pain should not be allowed to have a dog, let alone train one.

You can use a prong collar and get great results but you must understand how they work. The collar works because there are multiple contact points around the dog's neck. When a dog pulls, the contact points are distributed evenly making it uncomfortable for the dog to continue pulling.

WHAT ABOUT CHOKE COLLARS?

Pulling is the main reason people try different collars on their dogs. The oldest, most well-known collar is the choke collar. It has been used for decades by dog trainers and in my opinion, is very difficult to learn how to use the correct way. Most of the time it is put on wrong and in order to use the chain properly, it has to be kept loose around the dog's neck. When a correction is needed, there can't be any tension on the collar. You have to jerk and release to get any kind of effect. So since most dogs pull the second they feel any pressure on the leash, it is hard for anyone new to this collar to use it correctly.

There is a concept called opposition reflex in dogs. When your dog feels any pressure he will resist with counter pressure. So, if you push down on your dog, he will resist and push back. A collar and leash create opposition reflex, which is why it is difficult to get your dog under control when using a choke collar. A choke or slip is a good choice for dogs who escape from flat buckle collars, but for training, I think they are difficult to use.

SUPERSTITIOUS BEHAVIORS

As we discussed in Chapter Four, choke and prong collars in a group class can cause superstitious behavior to develop in your dog. He can develop an aggression problem by attending a group obedience class. Group classes are where the first-time dog owner will often find themselves. In many group classes, a choke or prong collar is handed out and the owner is instructed to use this type of collar to train. It's not a good idea to use these collars in a group setting. The problem is that they can create what we call superstitious associations. Your dog can associate the correction from the collar with the dog he may be looking at. Done enough times, and your dog will attribute the negative consequence of the collar with other dogs, developing a negative association, and becoming reactive in the presence of other dogs.

WHAT IF I FEEL BAD?

Reality can be tough to confront sometimes but there it is. You can face it or ignore it and pay the price. As Max de Pree once said, *"The first responsibility of a leader is to define reality."* I know the thought of bonking your dog will put some people in trauma. Others will shriek in horror. And others will say they could NEVER do it. I understand this. I see it all the time.

I was working with a nice couple that had a four-month-old golden retriever, a very nice, high-energy puppy. Every day this puppy grabbed and ripped shirts and had punctured skin with puppy biting and jumping. When I showed them how to punish using the bonker, the mom was shocked and said she could never do it and would not allow it. My response was simple. I told her I understood and asked her how long was she willing to have her clothes ripped? She wanted to know if there was anything else they could do. I said yes, you could put him in crate or tether him. You could also leave a leash on and use it when he starts to do anything you don't like. She told me their last golden jumped her entire life. They never got the behavior to stop. She'll have the same problem with this puppy because no amount of ignoring, redirecting, or counterconditioning will STOP this behavior.

Here's another way to look at it. Ask yourself this question. If you are uncomfortable bonking a dog, what about having his reproductive system chopped off (or cut out)? Sticking needles in your dog on a yearly basis? Combing out matts, ripping out ear hair, or expressing anal glands? Many dogs are routinely subjected to pain in the name of health care and grooming.

So, it all comes down to what behaviors you are willing to put up with. But it's completely unfair for the dog if those behaviors that an owner is unwilling to stop result in a trip to the shelter. I can guarantee you the dog would much rather have been given the correction and the chance to learn how to STOP the unacceptable behavior.

My wife Rachael and I have a great relationship because a very wise man taught me the secret to a good marriage. The secret is only one word. Do you know what the word is? I'll tell you in a moment. As a dog trainer, I have been in the middle of many husband/wife arguments. They have a disagreement about their dog and then turn to me and ask who is right. If I take his OR her side, I become the chump.

Dogs do a lot of things we don't like, just like our wives and husbands sometimes do things we don't like. A dog comes into the house and chews your favorite pair of shoes, pees on your expensive carpet, and digs a huge hole in your garden. We get mad at the dog and hopefully put a training program in place to teach the dog how to live with us in the house. We teach the dog our rules for successfully living under the same roof.

Success all comes down to communication. Communication is the training you use to teach your dog to pee outside and to chew on toys that you have given to him. Good communication between husbands and wives also goes a long way to create a happy marriage, but, there is also one more step that you need to take.

Forgiveness. You have to forgive your dog for chewing your favorite pair of shoes, for peeing on your expensive carpet, and for all the other bad behavior that he has done. It does NOT mean that you let your dog continue to chew your shoes and pee on your rugs. It means that you teach your dog the correct behaviors (according to you) and then forgive your dog. I know, it sounds metaphysical and woo woo, but I have seen people that are just constantly angry with their dogs and it's not a good situation. So the choice is up to you. Continue being mad at your dog, continue believing that your dog is getting back at you, keep thinking he was trying to spite you, or forgive. Move on, follow a training program, and watch your dog's behavior change for the good. So the secret to good relationships with humans or canines is simple… forgiveness.

CHAPTER 10

"Now here comes the big one. Relationships! We all got 'em, we all want 'em, what do we do with 'em?"

Jimmy Buffett

Exactly How To Develop A Rock Solid, Stable Relationship With Your Dog

Clearing Up The Confusion About Being "Alpha" And More

Let me share a BIG secret with you. When we think of dog training, we often think about treats, collars, leashes, clickers, toys, rewards, and punishment. But an important part of training has to do with the relationship between you and your dog. The relationship with your dog, or another person for that matter, is all about the interactions between the two of you.

In my first book, *"The Amazing Dog Training Man,"* I wrote an entire chapter about how the relationship with your dog works like a checking account. Every time you do something positive with your dog, you are making a deposit into the account. Every time you do something negative to your dog, you are making a withdrawal. In order for the relationship to stay positive, happy, and healthy, you have to be making more deposits than withdrawals. Too many withdrawals without enough deposits and the relationship will bounce.

Do you know anyone in your life that takes more withdrawals than makes deposits? I've had plenty of people like that in my life and I've learned to extract them as fast as possible. The last person who did this to me was quickly escorted out of my life. Your dog is stuck with you. Spend more time making deposits than withdrawals. It's fun, it's easy, and you and your dog will be much happier.

WHAT'S ALL THIS STUFF ABOUT BEING ALPHA?

The first canine term most people learn is the word Alpha. *"You must be your dog's alpha,"* some experts claim as soon as a new dog owner attends an obedience class. Others say dogs are not pack animals. Some even insist that we need to completely stop using the term Alpha. My opinion? If you like using the term Alpha or if you don't believe dogs are pack animals, it is all good with me. It's cool… BUT, and if I may say this is a BIG BUT - dogs ARE social. Some dogs are submissive, some are dominant, and some are in the middle. Observe a group of dogs for ten minutes and you'll see for yourself. Any social animal will respond to a structure. In other words, you'll have some dogs with a submissive personality, and you'll have some dogs with a more dominant personality. The submissive dogs will defer to the more dominant dogs, but here is the important point to remember: Behavior is always in a CONSTANT state of flux. Sometimes a submissive dog will challenge the dominant dog.

My very submissive Great Dane's name was Quinn. My very dominant Belgian malinois was named Suede. If Quinn was lying on the couch, he would refuse to move for Suede. Why did this happen? Isn't the submissive dog supposed to do everything the dominant dog wants? Not really. He gave in for pretty much everything else, but Quinn was one lazy dog and he held fast on the couch. My point is you need to think status more than being Alpha. Position yourself as the one who controls the activities which are important to your dog. Control the food, play, sleeping areas, and social contact.

The subject of dominance has been pushed around for a long time. What you need to do is establish a relationship where your dog understands you have the most status. The dominance model of behavior has been argued over and over among trainers and the consensus in the church is dogs do not have an alpha. I am not here to debate the argument. I am here to tell you after living with multiple dogs for years, I know from first-hand experience there is status. One dog will exert his status over the other dog. He will take the choice sleeping areas, he will take the toys, and he will dominate the owner's attention.

So with this knowledge you need to make sure your dog understands you have the highest status. You can take his food away, make him move off his sleeping areas, pet him when you want, and control his toys. Once you have established status it does not take much work to keep it. In the beginning it is important to follow some simple steps to ensure you are in charge. Most people think resources must be taken away from the dog. What really has to happen is resources needed to be controlled.

To establish your status, start including formal eye contact sessions with your dog in your daily routine. Eye contact with dogs always amazes me. Dogs use eye contact much the same way as humans. Dogs use eye contact to gain control over other dogs, think of the look your mother would give you when you were a kid from across the room if you were misbehaving. A submissive or insecure dog will have a hard time holding eye contact. Staring at a strange dog or person could provoke a confrontation. Do two or three eye contact sessions with your dog every day. It is a great way to bond and establish leadership.

As an added benefit, this will also greatly improve your dog's attention on you. Your dog will start to look at you when you say your dog's name which is extremely important for obedience.

THREE REASONS FOR PROBLEMS IN YOUR RELATIONSHIP

If you ever have a problem with your dog, you can trace it back to one of three things. You are having an attention, communication, or relationship problem. If your dog is not listening to you or not performing the command you are asking, there is a good chance your dog is not paying attention to you. The next place to look is communication. Communication is achieved through the use of markers so your dog understands what is expected of him. You can refer back to the chapter on markers if you have questions. The third place is your relationship.

CONTROLLING RESOURCES

The first step in establishing a good relationship is controlling your dog's resources. You can let him sleep on the bed, you can let him walk through the door before you, you can let him eat before you do. It is not a matter of taking resources away. It is a matter of controlling them. So when it comes to toys, sleeping, food, games, and social contact, you are in control. I will lay out each step but it does not have to be a super strict authoritarian type of relationship. You need to take control of a few resources and your dog will understand you have status.

I worked with a springer spaniel years ago that was getting aggressive. The husband worked third shift and every night mom would have the springer hop in bed and sleep with her. Dad would come home and the springer started growling at him. I was called in to help. I recommended the dog lose the privilege of sleeping in the bed. Mom did not like that advice so she didn't follow it which meant the dog kept growling at dad when he would come home. One morning when dad came home, the dog decided he was not getting out of bed. Dad reached down to try to move him and got nailed. The dog was put to sleep the next day.

That story was not to scare you, and letting your dog sleep on the bed is not going to turn him into Cujo, but it's important that your dog understand it's your bed and if you want, you can take that privilege away.

CONTROLLING THE FOOD

Establishing status with your dog is easy when you control the resources and the best place to start is with your dog's food. I always make sure the dog is calm and does not flip out when it comes to feeding times. A lot of dogs go crazy when the owner takes the food out. I always make my dogs do a short sit-stay when it is time to eat. I take the food bowl, put it on the ground, have my dogs wait ten to fifteen seconds and then let them eat. If they do not finish in about fifteen minutes or so, I pick up the bowls and put the food away. Handling mealtimes this way helps establish status and it is easy to do.

I am not a big fan of allowing a dog to free-freed (leaving the food out all day). I know plenty of people let their dogs eat whenever they want, but I believe it is better to manage the food so the dog always understands you control it. It is also easier to train a dog that does not have constant access to food. Motivation is essential when it comes to teaching a dog to do something. If your dog always has access to food, there is a good chance he is not going to get very excited about the treats you are using for training. When you control your dog's food, it will always help get a better response during training sessions. Training happens much faster with a dog that is excited and working for his food.

CONTROLLING SLEEPING, GROOMING & SOCIAL CONTACT

This is from an interview I did with Wes Murph, who is the only dog groomer to ever appear on The Dog Whisperer TV show. We recorded this interview for his podcast:

Wes: Excellent, so explain sleeping.

Eric: I would say eighty percent of dogs sleep on their owners' beds, furniture, couches, chairs, etc. even though most owners have been told to never, ever let their dogs sleep on the bed, or the couch, or a chair, and the dogs should always be on the floor. And I'm in complete disagreement with this. The only thing I say is if you don't want your dog on the bed or the furniture, then never allow him on the bed or the furniture. But if you don't have a problem with it, by all means let him up on your couch or your bed.

My dogs, I'm sure, are all on my couch sleeping and I don't have a problem with this. One of my dogs sleeps on the bed. She's a little Maltese poodle mix, and she's my wife's dog. But here's the thing, if you allow your dog on your furniture, your dog has to understand it's your space and not his and if you walk into the room and he's sleeping on the couch and you tell him, OFF, he should jump off the couch, or the bed, or the chair. You want to use this situation as an opportunity to let him know you are the one in charge.

It's very important you do this, because with a lot of dogs, the first place you'll see them react to their owners aggressively or start to ignore them is around the sleeping areas. So the owner walks into the room, will tell his dog to get off the couch and then Fluffy will give a little growl and you'll see some aggression pop up. I have no problem with dogs on the furniture, but you must make sure they are listening to your command OFF without giving you any lip.

Wes: And is it something a dog owner can practice at home? Like the feeding behaviors? Can you practice this when your dog is already on the couch and you ask him to get off and then let him back up?

Eric: Yes, and if your dog refuses to get off the couch, or the bed, or anything like that, I recommend putting a leash on the dog and what the owner can do is when he walks into the room, if the dog is on the bed or couch and won't get off, the owner can grab the leash and give the dog a slight tug to get him off the furniture. This way the owner can make sure his dog follows through and in a week or two, the dog will learn the word OFF.

Wes: You're not saying jerk the dog off the couch, but it's just a way to get this behavior at the moment.

Eric: Yes, I tell people to pick up the leash turn away from the dog and just start walking. The dog will follow.

Wes: What do you mean by grooming and social contact, Eric, and can you tell everyone how to use it to become the alpha in their dogs' eyes?

Eric: Sure, difficult dogs I have worked with, the dominant ones, are those who would not allow you to handle them and are very touchy about where they allow you to pet them. When it comes to nails, forget it, or looking at their ears. So one of the things I recommend is to start looking in the dog's ears. Look at the dog's paws, brush him. Start handling him and doing these activities, especially at a young age, because when the dog doesn't allow you to do these things, your dog is telling you to back off and every time you back off, your dog wins the little situation.

The steps I'm discussing are much easier if you start when you have an eight to ten-week-old puppy rather than a one hundred and fourteen pound Rottweiler. If I get a call from someone who says he has a two-and-a-half-year-old, one hundred and fifty-four pound Great Dane mix and is having problems with the dog being touched or handled, I know I have a real problem on my hands, because I must take some time to get to know the dog. I must spend some time getting the dog to associate his paws being handled and being touched as a positive instead of a negative, and this can be difficult when the dog has a history and has already formed certain opinions about the world.

So if you have a young puppy, now's a great time to start handling him and getting him used to his nails being clipped. Get him used to people looking in his ears, his paws being handled, all those good kinds of things. Because these are things you must do for the rest of your dog's life. And it's much easier to get him used to it while he's a puppy as opposed to waiting for him to become an adult dog when it's much harder to change his mind.

If your dog does allow you to do these things, great, but if he doesn't, then this is going to take some time, and sometimes this must be done in short sessions. Not too long ago I worked with an adult dog who didn't like his paws being touched and I had to hold a piece of liver on his nose or have a helper hold the liver on his nose while I reached down and started handling his paws. Sometimes I would touch his paws for just a second or two and then give him the treat. This had to be done over and over in order to get him to accept me handling his paws. Working with this dog just involved associating his paws being handled with something positive, over, and over, and over, until he would allow anyone to touch them because he already had a belief and some bad experiences with his paws being handled.

Wes: So you want to make sure you can pet your dog everywhere and he is fine with this. But what if your dog owner goes home and the dog doesn't like his ears to be touched? They have a treat again. The dog gets nasty quick, what is the corrective method at this point?

There are a lot of dogs who will use social contact to take control of a situation and turn it to their advantage. For example, a lot of dogs will go up to their owners and put their paws up on them while their owners are watching TV or drinking coffee. The dog is demanding attention, or social contact in those situations. It's a good idea to make the dog do something for you when he is demanding your attention. Because if the dog smacks his paw on your leg, and you give attention to your dog, you're reinforcing the idea that your dog is in charge and can get attention whenever he wants it. So, a much better thing to do with your dog when he is demanding attention is to give him a command like sit, or down.

Wes: So Eric, this is like when people come into my grooming store. Some of the dogs get excited and kind of jump up on their owner's wheelchair system, or the owner sits down and the dog jumps all over his lap. Is this a situation where an owner who has established himself as the pack leader should have a command like OFF, or SIT, or DOWN that the dog knows? It's not an appropriate time to jump on me and I don't want that.

Eric: It's great for the owner to have a command ready to give his dog when he takes him to the grooming shop or the vet's office. Those kinds of trips tend to make some dogs a little nervous, and it's always better to have something to give your dog to do than make a scene or injure you.

Wes: So let's talk about playing. What are some things we can and should do when it comes to playing? Tell us what someone could do for his dog's playing behavior so his dog learns the owner is the pack leader.

Eric: Okay, so playing, your dog Eliot likes to play right?

Wes: Oh gosh, he loves to play.

Eric: Right, right, and so do my dogs and so do most dogs. Most dogs love to play. It's what makes them so much fun to have as pets and so, if you watch a group of dogs or a group of puppies especially, you will see as they're playing they are communicating to each other. When we play with our dogs, we don't think of it as communicating with them, more like we're having fun, but they are learning a lot from us and our interactions with them.

So one misunderstood game is tug-o-war. Tug-o-war is a game most dog owners have been told to never, ever play and there is some partial truth to this. If you are not controlling the tug-o-war game, then you should not be playing it, but if you can control the game, it's one of the best games to play with your dog, hands down.

Does Elliott play tug?

Wes: He does, we have a big red rubber Kong which is so popular and I put it in his mouth and we play tug back and forth.

<u>**Eric**</u>: Right, so most dogs get excited and pick up the tug toy and the owner says, *"Oh look, Junior wants to play."*

So, he grabs onto the dog's toy, the dog starts to pull and he pulls, the dog pulls some more, and most dogs love to play for a lot longer than the owner wants to. So as the game starts, you and your dog are pulling back and forth, and you start thinking about other things you must do, you need to check your email, get dinner ready, etc. The dog is pulling on the tug toy and wants to play forever, but you have things to do so you let the toy go. Now from your point of view, it's not a big deal. But from your dog's point of view, it's huge. He is looking up at you. He's got his teeth wrapped around an object and pulling, trying to get it away from you and then you let go.

So look at what you're communicating to your dog. You're communicating you're weak when it comes to strength games. Your dog is also learning when he wants something bad enough; if he just pulls enough he can get what he wants. So this can cause problems because if you allow your dog to win the tug games, day after day, after day, after day, you are reinforcing how weak you are.

This can become a big problem as your dog gets older. Let's say you're in the kitchen and you drop a chicken bone and the dog grabs it and goes over to the corner. Now you're going to follow him to go get the bone back, and as you approach, your dog is thinking – *"You're not seriously thinking you can take this chicken from me? You lost three hundred and seventy-four games of tug-o-war and now you're going to try and take this away from me?* This is where tug games can cause some problems and if you reach down to grab the chicken bone from a dog who doesn't respond to you as the pack leader, you can have big-time problems. If you reach in, most dogs will growl to give you a warning and then if the owner growls back at the dog, and continues to reach for the bone, there's a good chance the dog will bite. Right?

Wes: Right.

Eric: The dog growls and then the owner growls back at the dog... So now we have a conflict. The way dogs resolve conflict is through aggression, so if you reach to get the bone, there is a good chance you'll get bit.

This is usually when I get the phone call asking me what to do when this happens. I always advise to back away. The best way to fix this problem is if you could go back in time to the tug games, and at the end of every tug game, instead of letting go and letting your dog win, make sure you win.

You say DROP IT and have your dog release the toy. Then you put the tug toy away until the next time you play. Getting your dog to drop the tug toy at the end of every game is crucial. Your dog has to hear the words DROP IT over, and over, and over until it becomes a learned behavior. Now, if your dog ever grabs a chicken bone, all you need to say is DROP IT. This is why I'm a big believer in playing tug games, because if you play often and if you win every game, this teaches your dog to DROP IT and release whatever is in his mouth on command.

Now, you've just established yourself as the one who wins the games, you're now developing a stronger position in the pack, and it makes your dog much safer because you now have control over the most dangerous part of your dog.

Wes: So Eric, I know tug is a popular game but there are other games like fetch and are you saying the owner should control all of the games? So you

as the owner should start the game and decide when to stop the game to teach your dog you are in control?

Eric: A lot of people play this kind of fetch game. The dog grabs the ball and comes back to the owner but he won't give the ball back and starts to run circles around the owner. Every time the owner goes toward the dog, he will jump back and play keep away with the ball. When this happens, your dog is learning he can control the game.

So now your dog is starting to learn he has the upper hand playing this game. This simple game can communicate the wrong information to your dog. An easy way to fix this problem is to always make sure you have two balls when playing fetch. With two balls, you can throw the first one for your dog and when he comes back with it but won't drop it, you don't chase after him. Instead, you stand there and pull out the second ball, but you don't give it to your dog. You start to play with the second ball yourself until your dog drops the one he has. This way you can turn it around and have your dog retrieving for you instead of chasing after your dog.

Wes: So what you're saying, Eric, is you want to be in control of the games. You want to start the games and you want to finish the games to teach the dog you are the pack leader.

Eric: That's correct.

THE AMAZING DOG TRAINING MAN'S GUIDE FOR A GOOD RELATIONSHIP WITH YOUR DOG

TAKE ACTION

One HUGE problem is waiting, waiting to train your dog, waiting to see if the behavior gets better, waiting to see if the behavior goes away. The best step is to take immediate action. Any behavior problems should be addressed as soon as possible. Left untreated, a behavior will become a habit.

Habits are much more difficult to deal with than a behavior which has only happened three or four times.

TRAIN YOUR PUPPY

Puppy training will lay a foundation which will last a lifetime. Behavior problems can be averted, obedience commands can be learned, and socialization will help the puppy become a well-behaved, stable, adult dog.

PROPER COMMUNICATION

Learn how to communicate to your dog. Training should consist of teaching your dog the words YES and NO. No harsh techniques are needed. Every dog can learn these two words and they can be used to teach your dog acceptable and unacceptable behaviors.

USE MEAL TIMES TO TRAIN

Most dogs are fed twice a day. Use this time to train and establish status. You can use your dog's food to teach the word YES and improve your dog's STAY command. Your dog's feeding schedule can be an important part of establishing a stable relationship.

GET THE GOOD STUFF

Feed your dog a quality grain-free dog food. A premium dog food will go a long way to improve your dog's health and quality of life. The grains fed to dogs in this country are a very poor and cheap source of nutrients. An overwhelming number of dogs suffer from allergies. I have seen many behavior issues improved with a change in diet.

STRUCTURED PLAY SESSIONS

A lot of dogs love to play tug, fetch, and chase games. It is good to play with your dog because of the bonding and exercise, but some rules should be followed. If you play tug games you should always initiate the game, end the game, always keeps the tug toy in your possession and teach your dog to release the tug toy on command.

WALK THIS WAY

There is a specific way to walk your dog. You need to do at least one structured walk every day. Your dog must walk without pulling or dragging you down the street. This is excellent mental and physical exercise for your dog. A Gentle Leader is a great way to prevent him from pulling and an excellent way for your dog to learn loose leash walking.

A few years back a lady walked into my office with two huge black eyes. She sat down and started to cry. I thought she had just been assaulted and I was getting ready to call the cops. Come to find out she was crying because of her dog. Her dog was a big, happy lab that was very strong and gave her the black eyes.

She was getting ready to walk her dog when she stopped for a moment just as she was going out the door. Her dog was already outside (on leash) but she was still inside the house. The lab saw a cat and took chase. She held onto the leash and went face first into the door.

She told me this was not the first time her dog had injured her, he was so strong and if she could not get him under control she must find him a new home. We took care of the problem in one session with a Gentle Leader.

TEACH IMPULSE CONTROL

Dogs do NOT understand delayed gratification. The front door opens and your will make a mad dash for it. Some dogs will knock the food bowls out of their owners' hands before they can be put on the ground. Teach your dog impulse control by having him sit and wait before entering or exiting the house, crate, and car. This will help establish control over your dog and increase your status.

ON OR OFF THE BED

There is a whole lot of controversy around letting dogs sleep on the bed or be allowed on the furniture, so let me settle it once and for all. Here is what you need to know: DO WHAT YOU WANT. Yes! Do what you want. If you want your dog on the bed, let him up. If you don't want your dog on the bed, don't let him up. As a lifelong dog lover, my dogs have always been allowed on my bed and furniture. I know people who would never allow their dogs on their bed. It's your decision!

What I do recommend is teaching your dog the furniture is yours and you give and take away permission. If your dog ever develops an aggression problem and growls while on your bed, the dog should lose this privilege.

NO JUMPING ALLOWED… EVER

The #1 behavior problem I see with most dogs is jumping. The jumping is usually taught when the dog is a pup because he is so cute. As the dog gets older, the jumping becomes worse. No one likes being jumped on and it can get a dog in hot water fast. A large percentage of the population is on the drug Coumadin or something similar. Coumadin thins the blood so anyone on it bleeds, sometimes uncontrollably, and often needs to go to the hospital for small cuts. I know dogs that have ended up in shelters and euthanized because they jumped. It's sad to think a dog would be put to sleep because of a jumping problem but it does happen.

M.O.B.

Management of Behavior is crucial when a dog first comes home. Dogs will chew, pee, poop in the house, steal, and more. Your dog has to learn the rules of the house and unless you can be with your dog every second, you need to think about managing your dog's behavior. A crate, baby gates, tethers, and X-pens can help you manage your dog's behavior. As your dog learns the rules of the house, you can manage less and less.

CONTROL SOCIAL INTERACTIONS

Dogs need social interaction and will sometimes demand it from you. Dogs will paw, whine, and bark to get attention. If you give attention to the dog he will become more and more demanding. If this happens, you can tell your dog to do a command before you give attention or you can say NO.

USE IT

Use your obedience commands in as many real situations as possible. Training should be incorporated in your day-to-day activities. Instead of setting aside time to train, do your training as you are interacting with your dog.

TEACH YOUR DOG "PLACE"

Train your dog to go to a place on command; it could be a bed, small rug, or towel. Your dog should learn to GO TO PLACE and stay there until released. This is a useful command and also helps establish control and status.

TEACH YES AND NO

It is essential to effectively communicate to your dog. Your dog will do behaviors you like and behaviors you don't like. You make the rules in your house. You are also one hundred percent responsible for your dog's behavior. Teaching YES will let your dog know what behaviors he can do. Behaviors like SIT, DOWN, STAY, and COME are YES behaviors.

Teaching your dog NO will let him know what behaviors he CAN'T do. In some ways, teaching your dog NO is more important than teaching your dog YES. This is because it is important for you to be able to STOP behaviors to keep your dog safe.

Follow the tips in this chapter and you'll be well on your way to developing a stable relationship with your dog. Training your dog requires communication, focus, and a solid relationship with you as the leader.

CHAPTER 11

"Facebook is not your friend, it is a surveillance engine."

Richard Stallman

What To Do When Your Dog Thinks You're Not Looking

The #1 Easiest Way To Prevent Behavior Problems

WHAT IS M.O.B.?

Supervision is important when you have a new dog in your house. A puppy needs constant supervision and will get into trouble if you are not watching every second. It's kind of like have little children. You literally can't take your eyes off them. Puppies will chew and eat anything they can fit in their mouths. They will pee and poop and ruin your floors as fast as you can clean up behind them. So, an important concept to follow is: Management of Behavior (M.O.B.).

Management means CONSTANT supervision and NOT allowing your dog to get into trouble. It does take some work in the beginning, but management will also make your life much easier down the road. A puppy can be put in a crate and learn to calm when he gets excited. Management is also the way you get the relationship started off on the right foot. When a puppy's behavior is not managed, the owner often gets frustrated and it is very easy for frustration to turn to anger. Coming home to find a pile of dog poop on the living room carpet, your favorite shoes destroyed, and the TV remote in a thousand pieces on the floor is a pretty quick way to see red. Trust me, it's much easier to manage your pup's behavior and confine him to a crate.

WHY M.O.B IS SO IMPORTANT

Crates are an important tool for you and your dog. Even if you don't like the thought of it, even if you think you would never use one, you should still crate train your dog. At some point in your dog's life, there is a good chance he will have to go into a crate. If your dog requires regular grooming, he must go into a crate. If you have to travel with your dog and when your dog goes to the vet, he will be required to go into a crate. It's much easier to crate train if you get your dog used to the crate when he is young.

I was once called to help a very nice retired couple with their West Highland terrier. They didn't like the thought of crate training, so they never did. All was fine for the first three years. They summered in Massachusetts and like half the population in the northeast; they went to Florida for the winter. They would drive down every year and there were no problems. After three years though, the husband experienced some medical problems and could no longer make the long drive. They had to start flying, which required their dog to get into a crate. Being a terrier, this strong-willed, little dog decided she would have nothing to do with it. I got the call about two weeks before their flight was scheduled to leave and we were able to crate train her, but it did take some work.

M.O.B. CAN SAVE YOUR DOG'S LIFE

The subject of confinement is upsetting to some and the thought of their dogs inside crates can be uncomfortable. The reality though is it is the best way to save your dog's life. As a former Animal Control Officer for the city of Fall River, Massachusetts, I saw a lot of unfortunate situations. Dogs got injured or killed because they were allowed too much freedom. Puppies seem to be on a constant mission to commit suicide. They are always eating and chewing on stuff which could injure or kill them. Instead of thinking about management as punishment, think of it as a way to keep your dog safe until you can supervise and monitor his behavior.

THE EAGLE EYE RULE

Have you ever noticed the Eye of Providence on the dollar bill? It is the all-knowing, all-seeing eye that is also displayed on the seal of the United States. I like to use this as an example of what life should seem like for your dog. Your dog should think you are ALWAYS watching. You should seem like the All Seeing Eye, especially when a dog or puppy first comes into your house. You should appear to be omnipresent.

This is kind of like when you were a kid and your mother would yell at you from the other room just as you were trying to sneak a cookie out of the jar. How did she do that?

Anyway, your dog has to think you always know what he is doing. This way you'll gain control over your dog and it will help when you start teaching commands like STAY and go out of your dog's sight. If he starts to move and you reappear the second that happens, he will start to behave when you are present, and when you not. The All Seeing Eye theory can be applied by using good management and making sure you are always supervising your dog. This theory has gotten much easier to implement over the years with the use of cell phones and small video cameras. You can easily set up a camera and watch your dog from a distance.

TOO MUCH FREEDOM

I started working with a new client. This puppy was having some problems. Housetraining was one of them. The other problem was the puppy was getting into things, grabbing the socks out of the laundry basket, biting the pant legs of the owner, knocking the garbage can over, jumping on the counters and coffee table, you know, typical puppy hijinks.

The exasperated owner said to me, *"I couldn't sit down and watch Jeopardy! This dog has me moving constantly and I can't get a second's rest,"* She added it was easier raising her kids than it was this puppy.

As a newly minted father of two, I agreed in and said it is harder because she is giving her pup way, way too much freedom. Small children require constant attention and supervision. A puppy does too… but with puppies, we have tools to manage their behavior. In my experience, new puppy owners don't do enough to manage behavior. I have one hard and fast rule for ALL puppy or newly adopted dog owners.

ALL FREEDOM IS EARNED

It is earned over time as the dog learns who the leader is. It is earned as the dog learns the rules of the house. No chewing, no peeing on the carpet, no stealing food off the counters, no jumping on the guests, etc. Managing your dog's behavior is easy. It is accomplished with crates, baby gates, leashes, and x-pens.

One of the most useful management techniques is tethering. Secure the leash to something study in the room, a door knob, a sturdy chair, or anything solid. With your dog tethered, he can be in the same room with you but he doesn't have total freedom. You can sit there and watch Jeopardy, Seinfeld, or the Patriots game without your dog pestering you or getting into trouble. It's simple, but one of the most important steps to having a puppy.

HOW TO TEACH YOUR DOG TO LOVE THE CRATE

We've already established the crate is a crucial component for managing behavior, keeping your dog safe, and to the housetraining process by helping your dog learn the right location for eliminating. The big problem is crate training is often taught with force which can set up a lifetime of stress for your dog every time he needs to go into one. Instead, by following a few simple steps, your dog can learn to love the crate. Here is how you can teach your dog to love the crate:

1. The first step is to think a little like your dog. Your dog does not want to go into the crate because he does not want his freedom taken away. Given a choice, your dog would be much happier chewing on the corners of your coffee table than stuck in a crate. Knowing this, if you force your dog into the crate, he will make negative connections and will resist every time you attempt to put him into it.

2. The next step is to build desire in your dog. How can you get it so your dog is fighting to get into the crate? Start with a Kong toy (available at any pet store). A Kong toy is a hard rubber toy with a hollow center. With your dog in front of his crate, you are going to stuff the Kong toy right in front of him. Put a generous portion of peanut butter or cream cheese in the Kong with his nose inches from it. Then place some strong scented liver or bacon treats into the Kong. Now you have a stuffed Kong your dog wants.

3. Your dog will be very excited at the prospect of getting a bacon and cheese stuffed Kong toy. At this point, throw the Kong into the crate but you are NOT going to let him get it. You are going to close the crate door as soon as you throw the cheese-stuffed Kong into the crate. Now your dog is on the outside looking in. He wants the Kong, but it is on the other side of the door.

4. This is where you start to build desire. Don't open the door right away. Wait a few seconds. Wait until your dog paws at the crate and whines a little. Wait a few more seconds and then let him into the crate to get the toy.

5. Repeat this exercise a few times a day. If your dog knows he is going to get the Kong, he will try harder and harder each time. Just like if you open the crate door when your dog is barking, he will learn the louder and longer he barks, you'll break down and let him out. Don't close the crate door when your dog goes in and grabs the Kong. Let him take it out. If you close the crate door on your dog, he may not go in again. You need him to make the decision to stay in the crate on his own. How do you do this? Simple, read on to the next step.

6. You now want to secure the Kong toy inside the crate. You want your dog to go into the crate but not leave with the toy. This can be accomplished by tying a string around the Kong and tying it to the back of the crate. Now when your dog goes into the crate and can't leave with the Kong, he has to lie down inside the crate to get the goodies. Once he does this, then you can start to close the crate door.

The first time you close the crate door, don't secure it. If your dog turns around and hits the door it should open. After a few days you can start to secure the door for a few minutes at a time.

Teaching your dog to love the crate takes time. It can backfire on you if you rush the process. Taking a few days to teach your dog to enjoy his crate is well worth it.

BABY GATES AND X-PENS

Management of behavior is not just using a crate. I leave a leash on the pup and I also use baby gates and x-pens. A baby gate helps me keep the dog in the room with me which is crucial when you are housetraining because you must have a constant visual on your puppy. An x-pen is similar to the pens kids are put in so you can do the dishes or laundry. The x-pen allows the dog to be in the room with you but have more space than in a crate. You can also use it to start teaching polite greetings. The x-pen has no top so you can reach over and pet your pup. You can start teaching greeting by walking up to the x-pen and only giving attention for sitting and calm behavior. If your puppy is excitable and jumps, walk away or ignore him. I love using x-pens for this reason.

Getting your dog used to only earning your attention when he is calm is a great habit to establish. The reverse is what usually happens. The dog is jumping, barking, nipping, and the owner either gives attention or encourages it. This is setting the puppy up for failure down the road when the little guy becomes a big guy and you must fight him off. It is much better to get your pup in the habit of receiving your attention only when he is calm.

UMBILICAL CORD TRAINING

I write a weekly dog training email newsletter that is sent to thousands of dog owners all over the world. A question came into ADTM central yesterday.

"Hi Eric, I really enjoy receiving your emails :) However, I didn't understand some of the suggestions in the last one; what is an "x-pen" and "umbilical cord training"?

Thank you so much,
Angela

Good question Angela. To catch you up to speed, I was discussing housetraining and taking small, one percent steps to solve any behavior problem or teach any command. You can read the entire email on my blog: EricLetendre.com/blog.

In it I listed some steps you could follow for housetraining and I mentioned x-pens and umbilical cord training. An X-pen is just a small fenced in area. It is great for puppies because there is more space than a crate but it still keeps your dog confined and is a great tool to manage your dog's behavior.

Umbilical cord training is tying a leash around your waist and attaching it to your dog. Now wherever you go, your dog goes too. If he starts to pee or poop, you just start heading for the door.

HOW TO INTRODUCE FREEDOM

Introducing freedom can be started as your dog gets a little older. I usually wait until the pup is at least ten months old. This is not a hard and fast rule, just what I do as he gets older and more mature. It's important to remember the All Seeing Eye theory and watch your pup closely when you first give him some freedom. Around ten months of age I will start giving a little freedom. At first I will leave the dog out of the crate and walk out the door. I want to set up a place where I can watch from outside so I can monitor what the pup is doing.

You can now set up a cell phone or cheap camera and watch your pup from outside your house or from the other room. If he gets into trouble, you know you need to continue with the crate and keep managing his behavior. If your pup does not get into trouble you can see how he does for ten minutes and then reenter. I work up to a half hour over the course of a week or two. If he is doing well, I keep increasing the time. I want to work up to where I can leave my dog out of the crate all the time. I only like to use the crate for as long as necessary. I love when my dogs get to the point where they can stay in the house unsupervised and I have no worries about a couch being chewed up or a turd left on the floor.

DOGS WILL BACKSLIDE

Backsliding is a normal, natural part of giving your dog freedom. At some point, your dog may chew something or have an accident. This could happen for different reasons. As your dog is getting older and maturing, something may have happened which frightened him or something may be stressing your dog. It is natural to backslide. What is important is to go back to managing a little more. If you see your dog starting to blow it, for whatever reason, just go back to using the crate a little more. Don't allow as much freedom.

You'll often see a dog backslide when something big happens in the house. When you move, if someone dies, a divorce, the loss of a job, a new baby, or anything else which can spike the stress level in the home may cause a backslide in behavior. Instead of getting upset with your dog, just start using the crate again and try to increase his exercise. Also, do some obedience and trick training with him. This will mentally and physically keep your dog active.

CHAPTER 12

"Sleeping dogs never get into trouble."

Unknown

The Simple Reason Dogs Were Better Behaved 100 Years Ago

Follow These Two Steps For A Better Behaved Dog

It all began in 1988, the year I started working with dogs in Hartford, Connecticut. It was one of the best decisions I ever made because I have been training dogs ever since and over the years, I have met and worked with thousands of dogs and their owners. Being a dog trainer is a great profession. You get to meet so many fantastic people and their dogs. So many stand out, and I remember many of the dogs I've worked with, but there is one who tops them all and his stories still bring a smile to my face, Decker, the yellow lab.

Decker had all the great qualities labs are famous for. One of my favorite Decker stories involved a Thanksgiving dinner and a very expensive tree.

You see, Decker was put outside during dinner because he was just being Decker. He was not content hanging on the porch all by himself so what did this brilliant lab do? He looked around the back deck and saw something which must have sparked his active canine brain. What he saw had very high worth to the humans on the other side of the glass door.

He walked up to a very old, very valued bonsai tree. He wrapped his mouth around the base of it and began running back and forth in front of the sliding glass door, in plain view of the entire family that had just sat down to a delicious Thanksgiving dinner. Needless to say, the feast was put on hold as everyone jumped up and took off in hot pursuit after Decker.

Decker had trained everyone to play on his terms. Decker loved training his family and was very good at it. It wasn't just his family; Decker was even good at training me. Decker had a wonderful lab face with huge black eyes which melted away any upset feelings you may have had. One time, when I wasn't paying attention, he bit though his leash and took off. Forty-five minutes later when I caught him, he used his big, happy lab face on me.

Decker kept me on my toes. Which leads me to a little dog trainers "inside baseball" for you.

One of the main reasons dogs have behavior problems is they have a lot of pent up physical energy. A dog that has too much mental or physical energy will get into trouble and it is not his fault. Decker had tons of energy and you were in big trouble if you did not give him enough exercise… mental and physical.

IMPORTANCE OF EXERCISE

Exercise is not the answer to all of your problems, but making sure your dog has an adequate supply is a good start. Without exercise, your dog will go a little nuts. Have you ever sat inside the house for two or three days? After even one day, I find myself going out of my mind. I must get out and see some people and do something. Your dog is the same way. He needs to get out and sniff things and see things and move around. A dog that is confined to a crate all day needs to get off the property and exercise.

Dogs today spend a lot of time in their crates because what other choice do the owners have? If they leave their dogs out of the crate, something will get destroyed. If this continues, the dogs will be taken to shelters or rehomed. Often, the owner does not want to give up on the dog but you can only replace the couch so many times. It is much better to use a crate for as long as you need in the beginning and then wean your dog off of it. When a crate does need to be used for hours every day, the owner has to make sure he takes some time to mentally and physically exercise his dog. Walks are great but running is even better, and a dog that likes to retrieve makes it pretty simple. You can stand in one spot and run your dog until he's good and tired.

THE ROLE OF DOGS HAS CHANGED

I would say less than three percent of the dogs I work with do what they were originally bred for. It is very rare for me to work with a border collie or sheltie that goes out every day and herds sheep. I don't know any Australian cattle dogs that herd cattle. Most labs and pointers don't hunt with their owners. None of the hounds I have worked with do scent work. My point is one hundred years ago, a dog had a defined role to follow. They were bred to perform specific tasks. Dogs were bred to hunt, herd, and guard. The majority of dogs today do nothing close to what they were bred for in the past. But even if your border collie never herds a flock of sheep, he still has all the same drives and a strong desire to work. Your job is to provide outlets for sufficient exercise and mental stimulation. This is why it so important to let certain breeds run and swim.

Companionship is pretty much all we ask of our dogs today. Most breeds, no matter what they were bred for in the past, are chosen because the owner likes the way they look. Since roles have changed, you must make sure the dog gets enough exercise to stay calm in the house. This is the reason dog daycare has become so popular over the years. Daycares have flourished because there is a huge need for them.

I started my first dog daycare in 1995 in Fall River, Massachusetts. Because it is such a blue collar city, no one thought it would work. I started it because one of my dog training clients had a Dalmatian he was ready to give up on. Every day he would come home and do his best to give his dog enough exercise. This Dalmatian had unlimited amounts of energy and nothing seemed to work so I asked him to leave his dog with me for the day. I let his dog play with my two dogs the entire day. The next day, the Dalmatian's owner came in and asked what I did to his dog. I thought he was upset with me. Instead, he said it was the first night in a long time he actually enjoyed being with his dog. His dog ate dinner and curled up on the couch next to him. He said it was well worth whatever price to bring his dog in for exercise a few times a week. Once his dog's energy was lowered, he was much more enjoyable to be around.

HOW TO LIVE WITH YOUR DOG

"Sleeping dogs never get into trouble," is a quote I always share with dog owners. Another popular quote is, *"The only good dog is a tired dog."* There is some truth to that, but my dogs are also good out on a walk and other places. It would be more accurate to say, *"The only good dog is a trained dog."* Anyway, training and exercise are very important for your dog. Combine the two and you will have a great companion. It is important to remember a dog with too much pent up energy will almost always manage to get into trouble.

Years ago, when I was still working animal control, I got a call from a lady that had a border collie with a chewing problem. She said the chewing was a big problem and it was costing her money. She asked if I could set up an appointment quickly. Sure, I know how it is. You come home and find your shoes chewed up, it can get annoying. I had no idea how bad this dog's chewing problem was. You see, this dog didn't have a chewing problem, he had a destruction problem.

When I arrived at the house, the nice lady showed me around her apartment. She then took me into one room where her dog had actually chewed a hole in the wall and went into the neighbor's apartment and chewed his stuff. Expensive? No kidding.

Come to find out her, her border collie was spending long hours alone and was getting very little exercise so most of my advice was focused on one thing - EXERCISE. Whenever your dog is having a behavior problem, the first place to start is with exercise. Once the dog was getting enough regular exercise, we started a behavior program, taking steps to teach new behaviors.

TWO TYPES OF EXERCISE EVERY DOG NEEDS

Every dog needs both physical and mental exercise, but this shouldn't turn into a part time job. When you provide your dog with physical and mental exercise, he will be much easier to live with. A combination of the two will calm your dog down and he will not be bouncing off the ceiling every time you come home.

You can start by doing some simple activities. Walking is good physical exercise for your dog but even more importantly, walking is great mental stimulation. This is the main reason you should try to walk your dog every day. This will give your dog a chance to see and smell different things, which is so important. There are some trainers who tell you a dog needs to be walked two to three hours a day. Are you kidding me? This is totally not practical. Just do your best to get your dog out of your house and around your neighborhood daily.

If your dog seems to have high exercise needs, look into a dog daycare or a dog walker. If your budget is tight, you can always invite a friend with a dog over to play. Mental stimulation can also be accomplished by doing obedience and trick training with your dog. I always spend a few minutes every morning and night doing some obedience commands to keep my dogs sharp.

FORTY-ONE DIFFERENT WAYS TO PHYSICALLY EXERCISE YOUR DOG

1. Memory retrieve
2. Two person recalls
3. Treasure hunt
4. Service dog gofer
5. Hide and seek
6. Leg weaves
7. Weaving with ski poles
8. Agility
9. Digging for objects
10. Herding indestructible ball
11. Chase remote control car
12. Chase object on fishing pole
13. Chase light
14. Chase racquetball bounce back
15. Chase remote control airplane
16. Chase hose with water
17. Chase ball
18. Lure coursing
19. Swimming free

20. Swim next to canoe
21. Swimming relay race with bumpers
22. Water Kong retrieve
23. Jumping over picnic benches
24. Skateboarding
25. Flyball
26. Frisbee
27. Mt. Bike
28. Run through powder snow
29. Run through sand dunes
30. Sled dog
31. Treadmill
32. Run a race track
33. Jog with dog
34. Rollerblade
35. Backpacking
36. Carting
37. Skijor
38. Run hills
39. Walk/run stairs
40. Throw ball downstairs
41. Throw ball upstairs

When you live in the northeast (and many other parts of the world), it can be difficult to get your dog outside some months of the year. Here are twelve ways I exercise my dog in the house.

1. Treadmill
2. Tug games
3. Kibble hunt
4. Hide n seek
5. Stuffed Kong toys
6. Buster cubes
7. Trick training
8. Puppy pushups (sit, down, sit, down)
9. Retrieving down a hallway or stairs
10. Obstacle course, a couch, table, hoola hoop, box, and a chair can make a great indoor obstacle course.
11. "Find It" game
12. Obedience training

DOG DAYCARE

Observation is important when you are looking for a great dog daycare. You should be able to go in and see how the staff interacts with the dogs (and owners), know the ratio of dogs to humans, and be able to inspect at any time.

I opened my first dog daycare in 1995 in an old mill in Fall River, Massachusetts. The neighborhood and building were run down but inside, I had freshly painted walls and spotless floors. I also cut a section of the wall out and installed a glass window. This way, at any time, someone could walk in and observe what the dogs were doing. There was nothing hidden and I had an open door policy. This is important for anyone who offers dog daycare. You should be able to see what is going on. Today, many dog daycares have cameras in place with online feeds so that owners can log in and watch their dogs at any time during the day. This provides peace of mind and keeps the dog daycare staff sharp. I know if I had to choose from a dog daycare which had cameras and one that didn't, I would go with the one with cameras. I understand there is downtime and you can't be watching all day, but a good dog daycare would have that video feed up and running and available for anyone to watch at any time.

A WORD ABOUT DOG PARKS

Caution is the first word that comes to mind when dog parks enter the conversation. They have exploded on the scene in many communities. I think they can be useful but I also think you need to exercise caution. Here are my thoughts. They can be very useful if you go at six in the morning. At that time, there is a good chance no one else is around. You would have the place all to yourself and you could work on off-leash training. Dog parks are fenced in so this would be a great place to practice. If, on the off chance, there was someone there, you could ask them if they'd agree to be a distraction for your dog.

On the flip side, you and your dog could have a horrible experience at the dog park because not everyone there is courteous or conscious of what is going on around them. There are dog owners who will not respect you or your wishes. I can't tell you how many of my clients with reactive dogs complain that other people continue to walk up to them with their dogs, even after they are asked to stay away. So, when you go to a dog park, be prepared to encounter people who are clueless and completely oblivious to what their dogs are doing. There is also a good chance that dogs will gang up and bully other dogs; there are fights, and a lot of other potential problems.

CHOOSE THE RIGHT BREED

Research is very important when you are thinking about getting a dog. If you are looking for a purebred, you will want to get a breed that fits your lifestyle. Nothing is foolproof though. I once met a dog owner who got a border collie because she wanted a high energy dog. She was a runner and loved to hike. She got a border collie thinking this would be the perfect companion. The dog turned out to be a couch potato.

A lot of people adopt rescue dogs and much like Forrest Gump's mama said, *"You never know what you're gonna get."* It's funny sometimes how shelters match adopted dogs with new families. I have worked with quite a few elderly people who were told they were adopting a small dog who will never grow over twenty pounds, only to end up with a ninety pound out-of-control monster. One elderly couple adopted a "small dog" puppy and over the next six months, the dog ballooned to seventy-five pounds and was stronger than both of them combined. By the time they called me in, I asked if they wanted to bring the dog back because it was such a mismatch. They were already attached to the big dog though and wanted me to work some magic. We were able to bring his behavior under control and they were able to walk him but they would have been much better off with a different sized dog.

EXERCISE WILL NOT SOLVE ALL YOUR BEHAVIOR PROBLEMS

Problems crop up for a lot of different reasons. Some of those problems are just a dog being a dog. Over the past few years, exercise has been promoted as the end-all be-all solution to behavior problems. The church members think if you just give your dog enough exercise, all your dog's bad behavior will go away. This is just not true. Exercise is part of the puzzle and needs to be a part of any training program, but it will not stop common behavior problems. If you give your dog exercise, he will still get excited and jump on people when they walk through the door. He will steal your pizza off the counter any chance he gets, he will still bark, chew, and do all the other things dogs are known to do. You'll still need to apply a negative consequence at times and let your dog know certain behaviors are unacceptable.

It's easy to tell the difference between a behavior problem and an exercise problem. A behavior problem is anything that causes you to say to yourself, *"I wish this dog would stop doing this behavior."* An exercise problem is the result of being pent up for long periods of time. When that is the case, you need to give your dog some much needed exercise so his pent up energy doesn't surface as a behavior problem.

DOGS ARE MUCH MORE SOCIAL THAN SPACIAL

Space is not enough for a dog. Most people think if a dog has acres and acres of land at his disposal he will be happy and get enough exercise. The thing is, dogs are much more interested in social contact than they are in fields. Your dog would much rather interact and play with you then have access to unlimited acres. If left outside, most dogs will find a nice shady spot to sleep until the owner comes home if given a chance because dogs are social they want to do stuff with you. Hanging out in a large yard by themselves is not exciting to dogs. Playing with you is. Playing with other dog-friendly dogs is also exciting for them.

CHAPTER 13

"Happiness is a warm puppy."

Charles Schulz

Is There A Best Time To Start Training A Dog?

How To Bond, Build Trust, And Start Your Training From Day One With Your Dog

Hartford, Connecticut in the nineties was not Miami Beach. People didn't flood there for vacation, sightseeing, top notch restaurants, or much else. The north end was no place for a casual evening stroll with a loved, to take in the ambiance of the city, unless you were into shootings, drug deals, and possible stabbings.

This is where I was working at the time, doing K9 Security, and I had a few run-ins with the locals. A friend of mine, who provided guard dogs for businesses in the area (junkyards, car dealerships, etc.), told me there was a new way the local punks were killing dogs. They would take a sponge, soak it in gravy and then let it dry out. Once dried, they would throw it over the fence for the dogs to eat. The sponge would get consumed, enter the dog's digestive system, expand, and would kill the dog because of the obstruction. His job was to make sure the dogs he sold for protection would ONLY eat from their food bowls. Otherwise, his dogs could die.

This may sound extreme, but it is not much different than what I must do for new puppy owners. Puppies will chew through electrical cords, eat chicken bones, swallow socks, and more. If you don't teach them what they can and can't chew, they could end up injured or worse. It's ironic, but a new puppy owner's job is always trying to prevent the pup from committing suicide. They'll walk right into the street with cars whizzing past, they bolt out the door into potential harm, eat chocolate when given the chance, and will try to ingest anything even remotely edible, sometimes inedible.

WHY IS PUPPY TRAINING IMPORTANT

Training is important when it comes to a new puppy. The biggest mistake owners make is waiting until the pup is older to start training, because then bad behaviors become more established. You can prevent a lot of behavior problems if you start your pup on the right path.

One of the biggest myths is you must wait until six months of age before you can start training. This was true years ago when you had the old-school yank and crank trainers. Even today, a lot of these types of trainers still won't take puppies because their methods are too harsh. But done right, you can gain a lot from a well-run puppy class. Your pup can start his obedience, you can prevent behavior problems from ever fully developing, and you can get the relationship off on the right foot. When looking for a puppy class, you want to find a trainer who has experience with pups and knows how to stop behaviors.

A common misconception is you can never use punishment or a negative consequence on a puppy. This is not true. Trust me, a puppy that only has treats thrown at him all day long will develop into an obnoxious adult dog that will jump, bite, and bark non-stop. A huge misconception is that punishment can NEVER be used on a puppy. Throughout the course of your puppy's life, negative things will happen. He'll be exposed to negative experiences at the vet's office; chances are your pup will get stepped on by accident, and more than likely he won't like getting his nails clipped. The force-free church members will shriek in terror at the suggestion of using a negative consequence on a puppy. They'll tell dog owners that the pup will develop lifelong fears, phobias, and possible aggression. It's just not true. Puppies will get stuck with needles, most get spayed or neutered, and they all get disciplined by mom and littermates. The pup learns from these situations.

Nipping bad behavior in the bud will actually strengthen the bond between you and your dog. Every interaction between you and your dog helps develop the bond. Small, seemingly insignificant incidents will sometimes have big effects on your dog. Your dog will be much better off if he is exposed to small amounts of stress as he is growing.

LITTLE HINGES SWING BIG DOORS

There was once a warrior on the verge of conquering the world. He had an army of half a million men, which made Europe tremble. This warrior had Rome in his sights and was threatening to go after it. Pillage and destruction followed this man wherever he went and he was ruthless. The night before he was to get married, he died, not in a swordfight, not at the end of a spear or arrow; he died from a nosebleed in his sleep. Attila the Hun suffered from chronic nosebleeds. He got drunk, passed out, and choked on his blood.

The story reminds me of a quote from W. Clement Stone, *"Little hinges swing big doors."* One little nose bleed wiped out one of history's fiercest and bloodiest warriors.

Successfully raising a new puppy requires little hinges swinging big doors. What you do with your new puppy will have lifelong effects. Small, little, trivial events can have a lasting impact. The moment your pup comes into your house is the time to get moving in the right direction.

The first step for new puppy owners is socialization. The next one is preventing behavior problems BEFORE they start. You also want to start teaching basic commands using positive, reward based methods. Doing the right things now with your pup will have lifelong implications and determine how your dog behaves as an adult.

WHAT AGE SHOULD PUPPY TRAINING START?

As soon as the new pup comes home, he makes a visit to the vet's office and vaccinations are started. The advice often given is to keep him in the house until vaccinations are completed. Most puppy classes start with dogs that are ten week old. Eight to eighteen weeks is a critical period of socialization in your puppy's life. All animals go through a socialization period and it is important for their development.

When I was a kid, my brother and sister and I found a baby duck. The little thing couldn't have been more than a few weeks old and she must have been going through her socialization period because within a day or so she was attached to us. She would follow us around, swim with us, and do whatever we were doing. She was like having a puppy.

A puppy's socialization period is a time where you want him to make connections with you and other humans. A puppy left too long with his littermates will not make the same connections and will tend to be fearful or engage much better with other dogs than his human family. Socialization is important. The problem is most puppy owners are told to keep the pup inside and away from being socialized. There is a risk of taking your pup out and about before being fully vaccinated, but the rewards far outweigh any potential health risks and it is a good course of action to take part in a puppy class.

Dogs that are not socialized develop behavior problems and fears which can be difficult to overcome, especially if you hire a church member. If you choose to keep your puppy inside until vaccinations are complete, he has a much stronger chance of developing behavior problems from lack of socialization. Your puppy needs to be brought out into the world and exposed to people, places, sights, sounds, and smells.

The one place you must be careful is exposing your puppy to other dogs. If you are going to let your pup play with other pups, you need to make sure the other puppies or dogs do not become too overbearing or bullying. For once, there is something that the American Veterinary Society of Animal Behavior and I agree on. This is from their website:

> *"...the American Veterinary Society of Animal Behavior believes that it should be the standard of care for puppies to receive such socialization before they are fully vaccinated. In general, puppies can start puppy socialization classes as early as 7-8 weeks of age. Puppies should receive a minimum of one set of vaccines at least 7 days prior to the first class and a first deworming. They should be kept up-to-date on vaccines throughout the class. Veterinarians specializing in behavior recommend that owners take advantage of every safe opportunity to expose young puppies to the great variety of stimuli that they will experience in their lives. Enrolling in puppy classes prior to three months of age can be an excellent means of improving training, strengthening the human-animal bond, and socializing puppies in an environment where risk of illness can be minimized."*

YOUR PUPPY HAS TO LEARN TO LIVE LIKE A HUMAN

Information is what your little puppy needs, information on how to live with humans. Puppies don't exhibit human behavior and will never learn to think like us. This would be anthropomorphic which gets a lot of dog owners in trouble. When we think our dogs can think like us we start to give them human characteristics and behaviors. Common sayings are, *"My dog is trying to spite me."* Or, *"He is getting back at me for leaving him home all day."* This is how we start getting in hot water with our pups. Your dog is just being a dog. If he chewed your shoes it was out of boredom or his intense desire to chew, not to spite you. It is crucial for your dog to learn what behaviors are acceptable and which ones are unacceptable. The faster this is accomplished the better, which is why we discussed management, exercise, communication, and socialization. If you follow those steps there is a great chance you and your dog will have a nice long happy life together. If this is not accomplished, if your dog does not learn how to live like a human, his days are numbered in many homes. There is only so long a person will put up with a steaming pile of poop on the carpet. There is only so long a person will put up with the TV remote getting chewed, with food being stolen off the table, with clothes getting ruined from jumping. These are all very natural, normal canine behaviors, but definitely not acceptable.

PUNISHMENT FOR PUPPIES

This brings us back to the topic of punishment and puppies which will have the church members gnashing their teeth and pulling their hair out. Can puppies be punished? My answer is YES! You can punish your pup for bad behavior. Are you just supposed to sit there and let your pup puncture your skin any time he feels like playing? Some poor puppy owners put up with biting for weeks when it could be stopped in a day with punishment. And for the record, let me just say one more time: PUNISHMENT IS NOT ABUSE!

Punishment will not damage the relationship between you and your pup. If anything, your pup will develop a level of respect for you and know you have the highest status in the house. Puppies are portrayed as fragile and sensitive little balls of fur, but advising puppy owners to allow unacceptable behaviors is crazy. Puppies grow up into adult dogs with large carnivorous teeth and powerful jaws. To allow your pup to bite, hump, and jump, and do all the other behaviors humans do not like is crazy. And if you think I am a mean, cold-hearted person who hates puppies and children, just remember this. Puppies have their reproductive systems ripped out, are stuck with sharp metal objects, and sometimes must suffer in pain for weeks in the name of good health. If your puppy eats a sock and you rush him to the vet's office he is going to sedate him and then slice his stomach open to get the obstruction out. Once they remove the sock, they will stitch him up which will take weeks to heal. This of course will save his life, but it will also cause pain and fear.

Why can vets and groomers do things which are a thousand times more painful and fearful than what I would do to stop a behavior? In the name of health, all bets are off. Why don't these procedures affect the dog for the rest of his life? Why would a quick bonk or squirt bottle spray cause life-long, irreparable harm? My question for the force-free church member is this, *"Do you recommend NOT spaying or neutering? Do you recommend avoiding vaccinations because they will damage the puppy and develop lifelong aggression problems? Do you recommend NOT clipping the pup's nails because it is too stressful and will develop fear?"* I didn't think so.

HOUSETRAINING IS NOT A BEHAVIOR PROBLEM

Does your puppy pee or poop on your floors? You probably think this is a behavior problem, but I would tell you it is actually NOT a behavior problem. Before you think I'm nuts for making such a bold statement, let me explain a few things. Many of the activities our dogs engage in that we don't like are labeled as behavior problems, but the reality is most of these activities are not.

For example, if you were walking along a path and your dog picked up a stick and started to chew on it you would think it was no big deal. *"Hey look, Junior is chewing on a stick."* But when Junior comes home and starts to chew on your expensive oak furniture, it becomes a problem.

Back to housetraining, peeing and pooping is a very normal, natural behavior. Every living creature does it. It only becomes a problem when your dog doesn't do it in the right area. So, my argument is housetraining is not a behavior problem, it is a location problem. Thinking of housetraining as a location problem will help you keep things in perspective to train your puppy to go in the RIGHT location.

SEVEN HOUSETRAINING STEPS

Step 1: Understand puppy behavior

Puppies do not know right from wrong. What they understand is safe and dangerous. When your puppy comes into your house, he doesn't understand it is bad behavior to urinate on your carpet. You want to teach your puppy going in the house is unacceptable. You do this by catching him in the act - not after the behavior has occurred but while the behavior is happening. Punishing your puppy after the behavior has occurred can confuse him, making the housetraining process much more difficult.

Step 2: Understand your puppy's digestive system

His digestive system is much shorter than a human's. You have twenty-six feet of intestines; an adult dog has eight feet, so the whole process is going to happen much faster. It is also important to remember what goes in must come out. Some dog food companies recommend feeding a puppy four times a day. This can make the housetraining process very, very difficult on the puppy and the owner. I have always fed my puppies twice a day. You can meet all of their nutritional requirements and make it much easier to house-train on this feeding schedule, which leads us to Step 3…

Step 3: Develop a schedule

Putting your puppy on a feeding schedule during the housetraining process can make your efforts much more successful. A puppy who is allowed to eat whenever he wants will make housetraining very difficult. Also, developing a schedule to take your puppy outside will make it easier on you. I always bring a puppy outside within five to ten minutes after meals.

Step 4: Manage your puppy's behavior

One of the most important steps in the housetraining process is proper management of your puppy's behavior. In Step 1, we discussed catching your puppy in the act, not after the fact. Using a crate can help you when you are too busy to watch him. Most pups will not eliminate in their crates. When you need to go to work or must leave the house for a while, you can put him in his crate. When you come home, you can take him outside and not give him the opportunity to make a mistake in the house. Using a crate is excellent for young dogs.

At some point in your dog's life he must go into a crate. The vet, travel, and grooming visits all require your dog to go into a crate. It is better to get him used to one while he is young. I also recommend crates because as a former Animal Control Officer, I have seen plenty of young dogs who were injured – some seriously - because they were allowed too much freedom while unattended.

Step 5: Influence your puppy's behavior

Just as you need to catch your puppy in the act, you also need to let him know he is doing the right behavior. During the housetraining process, it is a good idea to take your puppy out on leash. If you let him out into a fenced in area and you are not there, you will not be able to communicate to him he is doing the right behavior. When your pup needs to go out, put him on leash and as he is sniffing the ground, say a command like, GET BUSY or, DO

YOUR BUSINESS, and keep saying it until he starts to go. Once he starts, don't say anything else. Once he is finished, praise and reward him.

Step 6: Proper clean up

When I am helping someone housetrain their pup, one of the first questions I ask is, "*What are you cleaning up the mess with?*" A lot of people get commercial cleaners at the supermarket. Many of these products contain ammonia. Ammonia smells like urine to your puppy. So, if your puppy pees on the carpet and you clean with an ammonia product, he will come back to the same spot and think a strange dog has gone on the carpet. Your puppy will eliminate again on the same spot to cover it. Nature's Miracle is an excellent product which has enzymes to break down the scent of urine.

Step 7: Get everyone involved

If it's just you and your puppy, this step will be easy. If your puppy lives in a house with more than one person, make sure everyone is taking the steps necessary to make the housetraining process quick and easy. The closer everyone sticks to the plan, the faster the training will progress.

WANT A CALM PUPPY? DO THIS

On a beautiful spring morning a few years back I found myself sitting in a small classroom listening to "The Evil Russian," Pavel Tsatsouline discuss flexibility training. There were twenty-five people in the room and they were all there to learn techniques Pavel used to train the elite Russian Special Forces Unit, Spetznaz. Everyone listened as Pavel shared his secrets, but one person, me, was amazed at how some of what he said applied to dog training.

Have you ever wondered, as I have, what makes such a dramatic difference in the way a dog behaves? It isn't always the person training the dog. The difference lies in how well the person understands a few basic dog training techniques. It's important to understand you do NOT want to reinforce the behaviors you don't like. One of the biggest problems for ninety percent of dog owners is jumping and unruly behavior. You need to make sure you are not unintentionally reinforcing the unruly behavior. When a friend comes over and your dog starts to jump, the typical scenario goes something like this: Your friend pushes your dog or pets your dog, while you are trying to pull your dog back and are yelling, *"Down! Get down!"* This all reinforces the unruly behavior. Albeit unintentionally, but it is still reinforcing.

During the seminar, Pavel made a comment which applies to all of this. As he was discussing stretching he used the term: Forced Relaxation. He added, only the Russians can come up with a term like Forced Relaxation.

It struck me because this is what you need to do when dealing with a young dog who likes to jump and become unruly. You need to force him to relax. The easiest way is with a leash on him. Here's how it works. When your friend comes over the house, before you let your friend in, put a leash on your dog. You then step on the leash to prevent him from jumping. With all your weight on the leash, you force him to relax before your friend approaches and gives him any attention. Your dog only gets your friend's attention when he relaxes. If he is too strong for you, find a place in your house where you can secure the leash to something sturdy, this way your dog is out of the area where he can jump and get unintentional reinforcement.

Forced relaxation is a great way to teach calm behavior. The calmer the dog, the easier and more enjoyable he is to be around. Your friends will like you and your dog much better when they come over to your house and your dog does not maul them. It's hard to believe, but not everyone is a dog lover like you and me.

WHY YOU SHOULD KEEP A LEASH ON YOUR PUPPY

Control is an important part of raising a puppy. Dogs are predatory animals capable of killing. So your job is to make sure you have control and the easiest way to establish that is when your dog is a puppy. A good way is to restrict his freedom as he is growing up. I leave a leash on the dog at all times until he gets older. With a leash on, I can tether the puppy to a sturdy object, I can step on it, or I can pick up the leash when the puppy gets a little out of control. As your puppy gets older, you can give him more and more freedom, but he has to earn it.

Do you think this is mean? Remember when you were a kid? Freedom had to be earned. I know I had to earn it. I had to go to bed at a certain time, be home at a certain time. I had to eat when I was told; I had chores to do, and so on. To think this is mean for a puppy is crazy. I once worked with a young couple and they had a pretty out of control lab mix. I recommended leaving a leash on the pup. The wife said she could never, ever do this to her puppy. It was mean and cruel. I told her she didn't have to do anything I said. I could only make recommendations and she could choose to follow them or not. It doesn't make a difference to me. I'm not the one living with the out of control dog. I can't make anyone do anything, but I can help raise a puppy that will turn into a great companion.

COMMON PUPPY PROBLEMS

Common puppy problems can be resolved with a combination of management, punishment, and exercise. You don't have to put up with months and months of behaviors that drive you insane. The steps I have outlined will make life with your puppy much more bearable.

I would recommend getting a crate, baby gates, and few good leashes. I would also recommend re-reading the chapter on punishment and how to apply it to your pup when he is biting, chewing, or jumping. Remember, there's no punishment when housetraining. Set up an exercise routine for him. Up until four and a half months, puppies tend to sleep a lot. Then some seem to drink Red Bull with an espresso chaser and have incredible amounts of energy. Dog daycare can help.

You can also start teaching markers and behaviors. Teach your pup to SIT, DOWN, STAND, STAY, COME, and WALK ON LEASH. This is the blueprint for raising a great dog everyone will love to be around. No one wants to spend time with a dog who is out of control and not well-behaved. And believe me; you won't get the results you're looking for by throwing treats at your pup every two seconds.

CHAPTER 14

"Nature is where the reality happens."

J.T. Abraham

How To Cure Your Reactive Dog

Does Your Dog Freak Out On Leash? It Does NOT Take Weeks Or Months To Fix This Problem

The Potter League for Animals in Middletown, Rhode Island is a great shelter, run by some really amazing people and they invited me to speak at one of their Pet Universities, which is a regular monthly seminar series. That night I broke the record for attendees, drawing a standing room only crowd. I'm the first and only trainer to ever do that at Potters. I'd love to say I was the reason for so many people showing up, but that would be incorrect. I was not the reason for the record attendance that evening, it was the topic.

You see, my talk was on reactive dogs, dogs that lunge, bark, growl, and are uncontrollable around other dogs, animals, and people. Reactive dogs have become a HUGE problem and many dog owners need help, which is why they came out that evening in droves.

That night I taught a very specific method for dealing with reactive dogs. I also showed the results from recent training sessions I had with ten different clients. You can see the videos for yourself on DeadlyDogTraining-Myth.com. Each dog was trained using the same method.

WHAT IS A REACTIVE DOG?

Barking, lunging, and freaking out on leash have unfortunately become very common behaviors. Many owners can't even walk their dogs down the street anymore because they become so out of control. In my experience, this is now one of the most common behavior problems dog owners face.

It is common for young dogs to get reactive on leash. As dogs get a little older and start to hit physical and social maturity, they may start to develop and use their natural aggression. Most of the time, this aggression is out of fear and the dog only wants to get out of the current situation. The dog owner witnesses this and becomes concerned. He would like to walk his dog down the street but he can't anymore so he avoids walks. Left unchecked, the behavior worsens. When the dog doesn't get enough exercise, other behavior problems crop up and from there things can spiral out of control very quickly. To say this behavior must be fixed is an understatement. There is only one way to do that, and it's not one of the church's many goofy and long-winded protocols that will have you spending months working with fake dogs in the form of stuffed animals.

WHY THE SUDDEN INCREASE IN REACTIVE DOGS?

There are two main reasons dogs become reactive. The first reason is choke and prong collars are still too popular in group dog training classes. If this type of collar is used for training, it should always be used in a very nondistracting environment, not around other dogs or people because the dog could mistakenly associate the stimulus of the collar with the other person or dog. A dog in a room full of other dogs, being yanked on a choke or prong, can and often does result in aggressive behavior towards other dogs.

Here is what happens. Your dog with a prong collar sees another dog. Your dog starts to pull toward the other dog to say hi. Since your dog is pulling, you do what is natural. You pull back and "correct" your dog. There's a good chance your dog feels the pain of the correction while looking at the other dog he was pulling toward. The feeling from the collar while looking at the other dog could cause your dog to associate the discomfort with the other dog. Your dog sees another dog and starts to pull. You apply another correction. Your dog makes the association with another dog. You are now wading into very dangerous territory because your dog is starting to generalize the pain of the correction with different dogs. Once generalization happens, watch out. You are in for a rough ride. Your dog can go from happy and dog friendly to an absolute beast on leash. I've seen it happen more than once.

The other reason for reactive behavior is unintentional reinforcement from the owner. The dog becomes excited and the owner tries to calm the dog by petting and maybe giving treats. Trying to get the dog under control he will say things like, *"Nice dog, don't bark, be a good boy."* As he is petting and trying to reassure the dog, he is communicating that the dog should be doing the very behavior he is trying to get rid of. It's not the dog owner's fault. He is only doing what he would to a child or other nervous person.

And unfortunately, hiring a trainer, more often than not, will make the matter worse. Most of the prevailing wisdom will advise to use "counter-conditioning" to help the reactive dog. Counter-conditioning is when you pair something good (food) with the sight of another dog. They also get fancy and tell the owner they will classically condition the dog to like the sight of other dogs. If you remember, classical conditioning is learning through association, think Pavlov's dogs. Pair a sound with food and bingo, you have classical conditioning. So, with a reactive dog, they are going to pair the sight of another dog with a treat. This will make the sight of another dog POSITIVE. Hallelujah! Treats at the sight of another dog, oh boy this will work. But it doesn't. Instead they increase the dog's reactive behavior because what is needed is punishment.

I've also seen people work for months with their dogs from a distance, rewarding for being under threshold. Then they finally get within twenty feet of a strange dog and it is back to square one. The dog loses it sending them both back to the other end of the football field and starting the process of rewarding their dog for not reacting all over again. I've seen dog owners do this for months and when they are ready to give up, they are often blamed for not trying hard enough.

Bunk! When your dog becomes reactive you must INTERRUPT his behavior. The second you interrupt the dog's reaction and get his attention back, you will have the opportunity to reward a different response from your dog. After a session or two you can walk your reactive dog right up to another dog. Sometimes you can even let your dog to the end of his leash and sniff the other dog. I know to some of you this sounds outrageous and you're convinced I am exaggerating, but that is why I record what I do, so you can see up close, real world results.

So the reason we are seeing so many reactive dogs is a combination of dogs receiving unintentional and intentional reinforcement resulting in either reinforced reactivity or cross associations. In order to overcome this problem it is much better to startle the dog and interrupt the behavior. Doing this will help you get control over your dog.

GOOFY TECHNIQUES AND PROTOCOLS FOR REACTIVE DOGS

In order to avoid the use of (GASP) punishment, the all positive, force-free crowd has come up with a variety of training protocols to sidestep the right way to deal with this behavior. Some of the big ones out there include: B.A.T. (Behavior Adjustment Training), C.A.T. (Constructional Aggression

Treatment) L.A.T. (Look At That), Click to Calm, and C.A.R.E. (Conditioning And +R are Essential), but the insanity doesn't stop there. The internet is flooded with a whole host of others.

Currently, the most popular is B.A.T. When using B.A.T., you must always work your dog "under threshold." This means your dog is kept far enough away from the decoy dog so that he doesn't show any sign of arousal. Sometimes, he needs the decoy dog to literally be a football field away. As you're training, if your dog goes over threshold, you've blown it. Once he sees the decoy dog and becomes aroused, he is taken out of the situation. So your dog sees the decoy dog, becomes reactive, and you run away with your dog. C.A.T. works by having the other dog move away once your dog blows it. Oh yeah, this will work great. You'll spend months and months trying to make progress and in the end, you'll still have a dog that is reactive on leash. L.A.T. works by saying, "*look at the dog,*" and when they do, you click and reward. This is classical conditioning (what Pavlov did with his dogs). The difference is when Pavlov was ringing the bell and giving food, his dogs were in a neutral state of mind. When your dog is lunging at the end of the leash trying to rip off the other dog's face, clicking and treating AIN'T gonna work. You must shut down the behavior.

The problem with too many dog trainers today is they WISH every dog problem could be solved with positive reinforcement, counter-conditioning, and desensitization. Think I'm kidding? Some of the methods I listed above recommend using fake dogs, working your dog at least a football field away from other dogs or anything which will make your dog reactive, may take MONTHS for you to get results (which you won't), and best of all… if the training does not work, IT'S YOUR FAULT!

I can hear Mr. Miyagi's famous quote from The Karate Kid. "*No such thing as bad student, only bad teacher. Teacher say, student do.*" Maybe they don't like Ralph Macchio. Maybe they disagree with the wisdom of Mr. Miyagi, I don't know. What I do know is if you have a dog who is lunging, barking, acting aggressive toward other dogs, you can't be fooling around with fake dogs. You can't keep the other dogs (or fake dogs) a football field away. You need to be able to control your dog when another dog gets close and is all up in your dog's grill (like on an actual sidewalk).

ICE, ICE BABY

Not one to miss out on all the fun, I've created my own neat little acronym for handling reactivity. It's a different approach though (and it actually works). When you follow the I.C.E. Method (Interrupt, Consequence, Establish), you let the dogs approach and once the dog reacts, (barks, growls, lunges) you INTERRUPT the behavior with a negative CONSEQUENCE. Once the dog shows an acceptable behavior you apply a positive CONSEQUENCE and use positive reinforcement to ESTABLISH a new behavior.

In my experience, I find reactive dogs have very little impulse control. They must be taught to calm down on leash. They need feedback from you that their reactive behavior is unacceptable and needs to stop. The second problem you have with reactive dogs is that they lose focus on their owners and stay focused on the other dog. You can use all the fake dogs, barriers, and distance you want. You can take the dog out of the situation when he barks or the other dog can leave. And you'll spend months, or heaven forbid years, with little to zero results.

SO... how do you help a dog that is reactive? YES! You are correct! You use a negative consequence to stop a behavior. I.C.E. is simple. It stands for both the name of the protocol and the steps to follow.

I.C.E. - Impulse Control Education

And the steps to follow are:

I - **INTERRUPT** the behavior (aggression, lunging, etc.)
C - Use the correct **CONSEQUENCE** at the right time.
E - And then **ESTABLISH** a new and acceptable behavior.

IF YOU ARE SPENDING WEEKS OR MONTHS TRYING TO FIX THIS PROBLEM, FIND ANOTHER TRAINER

Months of training are commonplace when you are working with an all positive, force-free type. I know of dogs where owners have worked for years trying to get control around other dogs - YEARS! And after months and months of training if you don't get the results you are looking for the trainer will not pat you on the back and say, *"Well Fred, you did your best and you just have a dog that won't come around. Thanks for giving it your best shot."* You won't hear that.

What you will hear is much different. You will get blamed for not hanging in there. You will be told you aren't doing the training right and in some cases you don't even deserve to have the dog. This is what happens when you can't make their training methods work. Instead of reevaluating and trying different options like punishment, which reduces or eliminates a behavior, the dog owner is told to keep slugging along. It's amazing it has come this far. So let's talk a little more about actually helping your reactive dog.

Juanita Torres (name changed) went swimming in Connecticut with her family one summer afternoon in the Farmington River. Something happened and Juanita was dragged under the water. No one could find her. Police and fire departments were contacted and still no one could find her. State police divers were called in and searched for two days. Still no recovery. On the third day, her family members finally found her little, lifeless body. They placed her into their van and drove back to the neighborhood she had lived in. A large group of friends and family gathered and followed the van to the hospital where I was working.

About one hundred and fifty people showed up with Juanita's family. Her body was brought in as the friends and family waited outside on the street. They were mad, they were angry the police did not find her body. They felt the police gave up on their search too early. I was the shift security supervisor for the night and immediately got on the radio and called for our K-9 unit to come over and provide a deterrent because the presence of a dog can calm an angry group of people like nothing else. The assistant facility security supervisor (my boss) found out we had a dog there and fearing a "Bull Connors" moment ordered K-9 to back off and leave the area. As soon as the mob saw the K-9 unit leave, complete chaos broke out and within seconds we were in the middle of a full blown riot.

There were twelve of us working security and in less than a minute, it was twelve against one hundred and fifty. Luckily, Hartford Police arrived very quickly, but I have to say, those few minutes waiting for HPD to show up were pretty hairy and I was not sure how it was going to end.

I've seen aggression up close with humans and dogs and here is what you have to understand:

Aggressive behavior works completely on emotion. The brain checks out and emotion takes over. The brain basically says, *"I'll come back later. Until then please don't call me because I won't respond when you're like this."* When you have a dog that is reactive on leash, the dog can become overstimulated. In order to help a reactive dog you have to interrupt the behavior. By doing this you can help rewire your dog's thought process. The biggest problem with reactive dogs is focus. They are so focused on the other dog you can't get your dog's attention to do anything else. But once the behavior is interrupted, you can get him to focus back on you. Once you have focus, you'll be able to help your dog in these situations.

OVERSTIMULATION

Overstimulation is an understatement if you have a reactive dog. When he is overstimulated, it is difficult for your dog to think and learn. Your first goal is to calm your dog down. In this situation, nothing works like the bonker. Before I use the bonker on a dog that is reactive, I introduce it in a much more controlled situation. I want the dog to be aware of what it is.

Remember in this situation, when your dog is out of control, your dog starts to become immune to pain. So pain is not the answer. But startling your dog will interrupt his behavior. Your dog will want to avoid being startled. Once startled and the behavior is interrupted, your dog will calm down. Once your dog is calm, you can start to teach him what behaviors you do want. I have seen dogs calm down and get under control in less than five minutes. Could you imagine a behavior you have been putting up with for years under control in five minutes? You can see videos of dogs I have worked with on DeadlyDogTrainingMyth.com. It's important your dog also understands the word YES when you do this training. Once your dog is calm you need to reinforce his calm behavior as another dog approaches. You can reward your dog for being calm and work on teaching a new behavior in the presence of other dogs.

SPATIAL AWARENESS

Spatial awareness is a term you hear a lot with kids. It is knowing your body in relation to its surroundings. Spatial awareness is a term also used with dogs that have reactive problems. Once your dog sees another dog, he forgets spatial awareness in regard to where you are and focuses all his attention on the other dog. When this happens, you can't get any information into his brain. Trying to hand a treat to your dog in this situation won't work and if he did take the treat, you would be reinforcing the reactive behavior. So treats are out at this point. To move away with your dog also reinforces the behavior. He is most likely operating out of fear and to move away will start to work as a strategy. Your dog will like the result but it won't fix the behavior. If the other dog moves away, your dog will feel he has chased him off. It will do nothing to change your dog's spatial awareness which is what is needed at this point. Your dog has to be more aware of you than the other dog. Trying to associate a treat in this situation won't work because your dog is in a very hectic, out of control frame of mind. Again, you need to bring him back to calm and get him to focus on you.

FOCUS

Focus is what we are after and is the reason I am discussing spatial awareness. Once your dog has been startled with the bonker, he will become of aware of you and this gives you the opportunity to communicate to him. Now your dog is calm and focused so communication can occur. Without following these steps, it is next to impossible to get a reactive dog under control around other dogs. Focus and engagement is what you always need in training. Once your dog is focused on you and is calm, you can switch to positive reinforcement and start to reward him as another dog approaches or walks by.

I would much rather put the dog in a little discomfort with a bonk and bring the behavior under control than spend months and months letting it gather steam and become a habit. Every time your dog sees another dog and becomes reactive, his cortisol and adrenaline shoots up which is not healthy.

It is much better to bring the behavior under control and get your dog to focus and engage with you. Once engaged, you'll be able to bring your dog anywhere. Wouldn't you rather take a few sessions using the right training tools and techniques and finally bring your dog's behavior under control giving him a better quality of life?

WHAT TO DO ONCE YOU HAVE CONTROL

Repetition and generalization help once you have your dog under control and are able to establish communication. It's best to begin with high value treats. Your dog is now successfully walking past other dogs so you can begin to approach and stop. If your dog does not react, you would say YES and reward. The next step is to help your dog generalize. I often work with dogs that get used to one dog and they become well behaved. The next step is to have your dog walk past different dogs. Once they become good at this you would bring your dog into a group class.

I just had a little twelve year old rat terrier come into my group class after doing a few private sessions with her. She is now learning how to behave and perform her commands in the presence of dogs of different shapes and sizes. It can be done!

Most reactive dog classes have bags and bags of treats. They have curtains set up to work the dogs behind. The dogs are kept at a distance. The use fake stuffed dogs. This will not help your problem. Your dog has to learn how to get up close and personal with other dogs. They must learn how to behave and walk past all types of dogs. Once generalization happens, your dog is on his way to being cured. And there's real opportunity for a better life.

MOST REACTIVE DOGS CAN BE CURED IN A FEW SESSIONS

I know this seems like a huge claim but I am confident, in most cases a reactive dog can be cured within a few sessions. It will take the use of punishment to get real results but remember, punishment is not painful or abusive. The reason I added videos to the DeadlyDogTrainingMyth.com is so you can see all the different dogs I have helped overcome this common and frustrating problem. The use of punishment is controversial and it shouldn't be. Some people learn to live with jumping, counter surfing, digging, and even chewing, but reactive behavior is very frustrating and stressful for both the dog and owner. Trips to the vet or groomers become like military expeditions. Reactive dog owners set up detailed plans to get their dogs into the vet's office. They often need the help of friends and the days and weeks leading up to these excursions are beyond stressful

IT'S YOUR CHOICE

I know, I know. I can hear the church members now. They are lamenting that this approach will have long-term side effects. The dog is going to suppress the aggression and it will resurface. Science proves it! Mr. Amazing

Dog Training Man is wrong and does not know what he is talking about. Here is my advice to you. The choice is always one hundred percent yours. I will not cram my beliefs down your throat. By now, if you still believe in the all positive, force-free model, you should put this book down and go work with an all positive, force-free trainer. But, if you've tried the all positive model and have not gotten the results you think you could, give some of the techniques I have shared in this book a try. Check out the videos on DeadlyDogTrainingMyth.com to see for yourself that the dogs are under control and have not become snarling, aggressive beasts because punishment was used.

CONCLUSION

"There are two ways to be fooled: One is to believe what isn't true. The other is to refuse to accept what is true."

Soren Kierkegaard

New York is a great state, full of wonderful places to visit and other than their football and baseball teams, I love New York. Here are some interesting laws which are still on the books in the great state of New York:

It is illegal to congregate in public with two or more people while each wearing a mask or any face covering which disguises your identity.

- The penalty for jumping off a building is death.
- A person may not walk around on Sundays with an ice cream cone in his/her pocket.
- While riding in an elevator, one must talk to no one, and fold his hands while looking toward the door. (They needed a law for this?)

- Slippers are not to be worn after 10:00 PM.
- During a concert, it is illegal to eat peanuts and walk backwards on the sidewalks.
- Eating while swimming in the ocean is prohibited.
- People may not slurp their soup.
- Pinball machines are not to be played on Sunday.
- Raw hamburger may not be sold.

I could show lists of weird laws in every state. Massachusetts, where I live, has their share of them but they got at least one right.

- Tomatoes may not be used in the production of clam chowder.

Now this is one smart law. What self-respecting clam chowder lover could ever eat a bowl of chowder served with tomatoes? It just goes against everything that is right and decent. I hope the penalties are stiff.

Anyway, why am I picking on New York? Am I still upset with the 2007 Super Bowl? The fact that Babe Ruth, Luis Tiant, Wade Boggs, Roger Clemens and Johnny Damon went from the Red Sox to the Yankees? Nope. None of it. I am writing about New York for one main reason.

On December 16, 2016 a Bill was introduced into the New York State Senate which would require licensing and educational standards for individuals providing canine training for non-police and non-service dogs. This could be a nightmare. A nightmare which results in the death of thousands of dogs in certain cities and countries around the world.

In Scotland, electronic collars have already been banned. Quebec recently banned all prong and electronic collars. These measures do not help dogs. In the long run, shelters will end up becoming even more overcrowded and landfills overloaded with the carcasses of the dogs that had to be put to sleep.

All the result of banning the very tools professional dog trainers use to help dog owners teach and train their dogs how to behave with a human family. The one person on the front line who can help dogs with behavior problems, more than anyone else, is the trainer who understands and uses all four behavior quadrants. A trainer who understands and uses a combination of positive reinforcement and punishment will do more to help dogs than the act of banning e-collars in every country on the planet.

Watch some of the great dog trainers of today using an electronic or prong collar and you'll see trainers who love and respect dogs; trainers like Gary Wilkes (who invented clicker training but also understands and teaches the correct use of punishment), Duke Ferguson, Michael Ellis, Forrest Micke, Tyler Muto and more. You'll see how careful they are when using these tools, how they gradually introduce these tools and slowly teach the dog the meaning of the stimulation. You can go to YouTube and see dogs working with prong and electronic collars and they are wagging their tails and clearly enjoying the training.

How can this happen? How can a dog with a prong or electronic "shock" collar be happy during training? Because when you truly understand how to use these training tools, you learn they are NOT about pain. They provide communication, the main point I have been making through the entire book. The current president of the International Association of Canine Professionals, Tyler Muto states: *"Use patience over power."* These do NOT sound like the words of an abusive trainer to me.

The reason dog trainers get nervous when politicians step in is simple. Politicians will listen to the "intellectuals." Organizations like the Association of Professional Dog Trainers and the Pet Professional Guild will scream from the rooftops they have science backing them up. They are the ones who are kind and would never use abusive tools like prong or electronic collars.

If this bill is passed it will not just regulate the dog training industry, it will open the door to outlawing important training tools. This would be a huge disservice to dog owners and the dogs themselves. I hope by now you understand using negative consequences and punishment is NOT abuse. Punishment is actually how you save a dog's life. We can't continue to put an ideology before the life of a dog.

The all positive dog trainers are hard-core ideologues. They are not just church members, they are RADICAL church members, or what I like to call RCMs for short. RCMs do not allow conversation. They have to control the conversation and anyone who does not conform is labeled abusive, uneducated, and unscientific.

Well, in the end the lawmakers will make their decisions but it is my sincere hope that they don't believe in what isn't true, or refuse to accept what is true.

Additional Resources

"101 Ways To Improve Your Dog's Behavior" - You can get this popular ebook FREE! Go to AmazingDogTrainingMan.com

Leash Walking Secrets - Struggling to get your dog to walk on leash? This step-by-step course will show you how to train your dog to walk politely at your side. Go to: LeashWalkingSecrets.com

Ultimate Online Recall Course - Scared that your dog won't come when called if he gets loose? Learn the secrets of teaching your dog to come when called. Go to: DogTrainingRecall.com

Dog Training Inner Circle - With over 90 videos, courses, and articles, this is the website to help train your dog to perform obedience commands and deal with behavior problems. Go to: DogTrainingInnerCircle.com

Eric Letendre's YouTube channel - With over 12 million video views, this is a popular dog training channel. Go to: YouTube.com/eletendre1

Eric Letendre's Facebook Page - Join thousands of dog owners and "LIKE" his page at: Facebook.com/AmazingDogTrainingMan

Downloaded Over 70,000 Times!

Eric Letendre's

"101 Ways To Improve Your Dog's Behavior"

Get It FREE!

You can get Eric Letendre's popular eBook,***"101 Ways To Improve Your Dog's Behavior,"*** FREE! Included with the 101 tips to help your dog are videos which will give you step-by-step explanations. Go to AmazingDogTrainingMan.com for your FREE copy. Here is what you'll discover:

- How to prevent up to 80% of your dog's behavior problems before they ever develop. (Once a behavior problem becomes a habit it is much more difficult to deal with. Learn what to do instead.)
- The forbidden game you should play with your dog every day. (This one game will develop and strengthen a bond with your dog, is a great motivational tool for obedience, and prevents dog bites.)
- The #1 best way to feed a hyper, over-active, easily over-stimulated dog. (This one tip can make your life MUCH easier.)
- The easiest four-step method for establishing leadership with your dog. (Leadership is crucial and easy to establish with this one tip.)
- Dog likes to keep the ball when you play fetch? Here's what to do. (This is the easiest way to teach your dog to "drop it".)

- How to read dog food labels and why to avoid any food made with "by-products." (And why you should know what "BHA," "BHT," and Ethoxyquin mean.)
- Why you need to go to your veterinarian before going to a dog trainer for certain behavior problems. (Learn which behavior problems require a vet check before training can begin.)
- Before your dog will ever learn to come when called, you must follow this simple step. (This is often overlooked and ignored but is crucial for your dog to learn this important command.)
- Step-by-step instructions and videos showing you how to teach your dog to come when called. (This technique is a very powerful way to teach this command.)
- And much, much more…

Get your FREE copy of "101 Ways To Improve Your Dog's Behavior" at:

AmazingDogTrainingMan.com

About The Author

Eric, **"The Amazing Dog Training Man,"** Letendre took his first dog training class with his beagle-mix, "Union," when he was ten years old in Glastonbury, CT. His professional career started in 1988 when he was hired as a security patrol dog handler for the St. Francis Hospital Security Department in Hartford, CT. Within two years he was promoted to K-9 Supervisor.

In 1992 he completed the Professional Dog Trainer's Course at Connecticut K-9 Education Center in Newington, CT where he received his degrees in Professional Dog Training and Security Dog Training. Upon graduation, he was hired by Connecticut K-9 and was quickly promoted to Director of Training. In 1995, Eric relocated to Massachusetts and opened American Canine, Southern New England's premier pet care facility; which offered training, boarding, grooming, and daycare.

Since 1995 Eric has continued working in many diverse areas of the pet industry including working as an animal control officer for the city of Fall River, MA, K-9 consultant for World Wide Plaza in Manhattan, NY, and K-9 consultant for Hartford Hospital in Hartford, CT.

He has provided training and behavior programs for many area animal shelters including Placing Paws in Tiverton, RI, Animal Rescue League of New Bedford, MA, Potter League for Animals in Middletown, RI and Forever Paws in Fall River, MA. He has also helped thousands of dog owners learn how to train their dogs and solve behavior problems.

Eric is the author of numerous reports, the E-Book, ***"101 Ways to Improve Your Dog's Behavior," "The Amazing Dog Training Man Book,"*** and produced and stars in his DVD, ***"Secrets of a Professional Dog Trainer.***

Made in the USA
Middletown, DE
22 July 2019